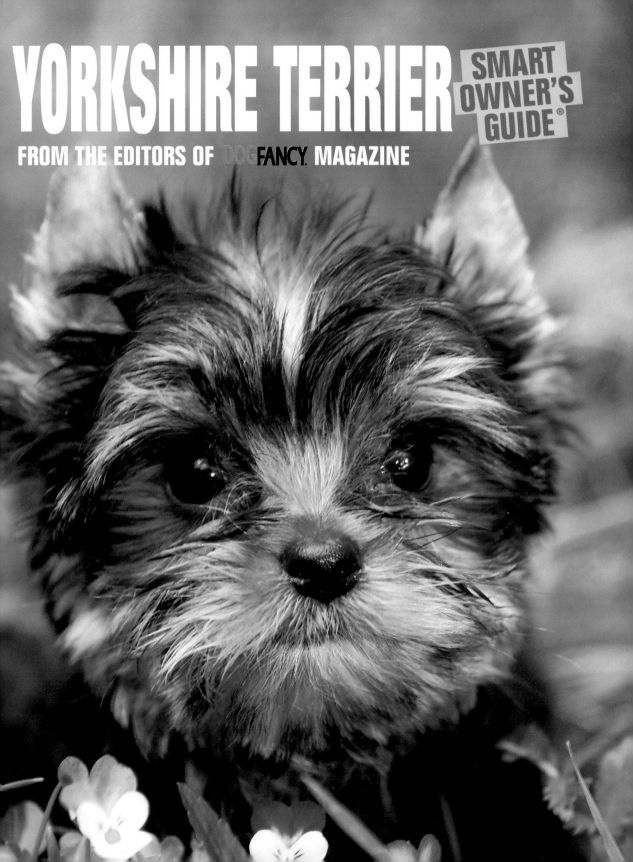

YORKSHIRE TERRIER

SMART OWNER'S GUIDE®

FROM THE EDITORS OF DOG FANCY. MAGAZINE

CONTENTS

Yorkshire Terrier, a Smart Owner's Guide®
part of the Kennel Club Books® Interactive Series®
ISBN: 978-1-593787-52-3. ©2009

photographers include Tara Darling, Isabelle Français, and Carol Ann Johnson

15 14 13 12 11   4 5 6 7 8 9 10

K9 EXPERT

Who can resist a Yorkie? This tiny toy dog is small enough to take just about anywhere. Tuck him in your bag, and you likely can sneak him into the movies, the library, even a restaurant. Not that we recommend you do. It's just to demonstrate how very portable this lively, gorgeous little dog is.

Weighing in at just under seven pounds and standing eight to nine inches at the shoulder, the Yorkie is one small breed.

Those of us who have been lucky enough to share our lives with a Yorkie know there's a lot more to this breed than meets the eye. It's small in size, but big in personality. The Yorkshire Terrier has no idea he's a tiny dog. He thinks he can run with the big dogs, and if you let him, he will.

If alerting his owners to intruders by barking were enough to protect them, everyone would want a Yorkshire Terrier. That's the terrier part coming out. After all, the

breed's first job was to protect farmers' grain from mice and other rodents. You don't preserve the harvest by being a wallflower.

Other terrier traits remain as well, including a tendency to chew and to dig. So, if you decide you can't live without a Yorkie, you'll need to give him toys that encourage him to gnaw appropriately and also provide an outlet for digging, whether it's a corner of your garden or a little sandbox all her own.

The other half of the Yorkshire Terrier is a loving lap dog. He'll be happy to keep you company while you watch TV, read a book, or create a lap for no reason at all. When he looks up at you with those sweet brown eyes, you'll find him impossible to resist.

Then when you're ready to go out, he'll be right by your side. You'll never have to take a walk alone or enjoy a lovely day sitting on the grass at the park solo again. Your new pal will cheerfully accompany you on outings, charming everyone he meets from the teller at the bank to everyone at the pet-supply store.

While you're there, stock up on a good urine remover. Yorkies tend to be a little tough to house-train, so prepare to make lots of trips to the backyard and to clean up a few accidents. Get a good brush, too. Nearly daily brushing helps keep that beautiful coat free of mats and tangles, as does a weekly bath. Or, if that's a bit too much brushing for your lifestyle, consider a shorter puppy clip.

Also, if you have children younger than the age of ten, put off getting a Yorkshire Terrier until they're older. These dogs are so small, they can be injured accidentally by a

With this Smart Owner's Guide®, you are well on your way to getting your Yorkie diploma. But your Yorkshire Terrier education doesn't end here. You're invited to join Club Yorkie® (**DogChannel.com/Club-Yorkie**), a FREE online site with lots of fun and instructive online features like:

◆ **forums, blogs,** and **profiles** where you can connect with other Yorkie owners
◆ **downloadable charts** and **checklists** to help you be a smart and loving Yorkshire Terrier owner
◆ access to **e-cards, wallpapers,** and **screensavers**
◆ interactive **games**
◆ Yorkie-specific **quizzes**

The **Smart Owner's Guide®** series and Club Yorkie® are backed by the experts at DOG FANCY magazine and DogChannel.com—who have been providing trusted and up-to-date information about dogs and dog people for forty years. Log on and join the club today!

child. In addition, the breed tends not to like little kids who move quickly, make lots of noise, and tower over a tiny pup.

If you've got all that covered, or you're already happily living with a Yorkie, congratulations! You've got a good friend and companion for years to come.

Susan Chaney
Editor, DOG FANCY

AN ENGLISH

Who can resist the charms of a Yorkshire Terrier? What could shake the blues from your lonely evening more readily than a blue and tan toy terrier? It would appear that almost anyone who's inclined to own a Yorkshire Terrier should do so! There are so many gigantic advantages wrapped up in this smallest of dog breeds.

As cute as they are, Yorkies really aren't for everyone, though. Surprising numbers of dogs are given up by their owners and end up in shelters and rescues. Yorkies are small in size, but they are large in attitude. But no matter how self-confident they are, they need constant supervision. They need smart owners to treat them as if they were larger (by not coddling them), while understanding that their bravado is mostly bluff (and not letting them challenge the neighborhood bully). In other words, Yorkies' interests are best served by those who see them for what they are: big dogs in very small bodies.

SMALL FRIES

Given the tiny size, the Yorkie doesn't impose upon your space. You don't need a palatial estate with a top-security fence. You don't need a large home to provide ample

Did You Know? Closely related to the Yorkie's big-dog attitude is his busy nature. As their owners put it, Yorkies are "into everything." A Yorkie who isn't pestering you to death is probably into something you'd rather he wasn't.

Yorkies are just like potato chips: You can't have just one!

exercise for the dog indoors. You don't need to stress your budget to afford to feed the dog. You don't need to purchase expensive equipment to train, house, and otherwise accommodate your Yorkshire Terrier.

You *do* need to open your heart to this seven-pound wonder and learn to give yourself freely and without reservation to another living creature. The Yorkshire Terrier welcomes everyone into his world. He is a trusting soul who shares his affectionate ways with anyone

kind and good-humored enough to spend time with him.

Yorkies like people most of all. While they get along with most other dogs, they are not clannish or selfish. Smart owners are advised to supervise the introduction of their Yorkies to larger dogs. Even though your Yorkie will not be afraid of a larger dog, such as a Doberman Pinscher or a German Shepherd Dog, the larger breed may not realize his own strength. Many Yorkies have been harmed by larger dogs who playfully mouthed them or pawed down at them. Once the larger dog realizes that the Yorkie is a member of his canine clan, he will want to "talk dog" with him.

Although not the size of a guard dog, the Yorkshire Terrier is most protective of his home and people. He still possesses all the fire of his terrier ancestors; he is fearless

it's a **Fact**

Tiny as they are, Yorkies make excellent watchdogs. It's in their nature to sound the alarm if a stranger passes the door.

beyond his size. A Yorkshire Terrier, whose temper is incited, will make quite a display of spit and attitude when protecting his owner's property, car, or home. Yorkies have the memory of elephants! Once you cross a Yorkie and he brands you as a foe, he will never forget your transgression.

For the most part, Yorkies love to have great fun. They are not vindictive, despite their serious ways during serious times. As with most other toy dogs, play is a way of life for Yorkies! Simple games, such as rolling a ball, chasing a string, or fetching a bone, make the Yorkie a happy pal to have about. His extroverted personality, coupled with his playful air, make him an ideal choice for young and old alike. Jumping about the furniture and leaping after imaginary mice and other prey, the Yorkshire Terrier can entertain even the most reserved of guests.

NOT KIDDING AROUND

Children and Yorkies are natural companions. Given the petite size of the Yorkie, caution is in order. Most breeders recommend that larger Yorkies (even in excess of the seven-pound limit) be selected for families with children. Because youngsters tend to be pretty rough on their toys (and toy dogs), they must be taught that the Yorkie is a fragile living creature. This is not a doll that can be tossed about with abandon. Yorkshire Terriers can be injured by excitable children who poke at their eyes or tear a ligament or break a leg by tossing or dropping the young dog. Yorkies have much to teach children in

They may be terriers, but these dogs turn to mush when they're in your lap.

JOIN OUR ONLINE Club Yorkie®

Meet other Yorkie owners just like you. On our Yorkie forums, you can chat about your Yorkshire Terrier and ask other owners for advice on training, health issues, and anything else about your favorite dog breed. Log onto **DogChannel.com/Club-Yorkie** for details!

terms of care, trust, and mutual affection. When properly instructed and supervised, this is a marvelous pairing.

"Yorkies can mix well with children," says Linda Grimm of Valrico, Fla., a Yorkie breeder since 1995. However, "I personally don't place a Yorkie in a family with children under the age of twelve," she adds. "Kids will be kids. All it takes is one minute for the child to stand in an open doorway to the outside and out the Yorkie runs." Grimm also believes that children may not understand that a toy dog cannot play nonstop like a large dog can, or that tiny puppies need to rest and recharge.

The American Kennel Club, in the 19th edition of its *Complete Dog Book* (Howell) rated the Yorkshire Terrier, as well as many toy breeds, as "not good with children." (The volume was later recalled when toy-breed clubs objected.)

This seems to be the critical factor. Dogs, like children, learn what they live. Yorkshire Terriers who grow up in homes with well-supervised, respectful children are likely to be comfortable with young children's shrill voices and sudden movements, and will

Yorkies take cuteness to a whole other level!

Did You Know?

The Yorkie is definitely a breed with more *chutzpah* than is warranted. Some behaviorists theorize that the Yorkie's extreme *bravado* is actually the sign of a dog who thinks he has to protect his owner, who all too often, because the dog is too little to take seriously, has abdicated the power position in the household. Fortunately, the remedy is simple: As long as the owner accepts the role of pack leader, the Yorkie won't have to, and this suicidal behavior may gradually become extinguished.

have learned to avoid being stepped on. Extremely young children, however, such as toddlers, haven't yet achieved the motor control necessary to avoid harming a small dog, even if accidentally. Toy dogs, on the other hand, frequently compensate for their vulnerability by adopting a defensively aggressive posture, such as growling, snap-

ping, or biting. In these cases, both child and dog need to be protected from one another.

Older people also adore the Yorkshire Terrier. This breed's entertaining antics and gentle ways make them suitable for the housebound and for those who are less likely to take their dogs jogging on the oceanfront. Yorkshire Terriers can receive ample exercise

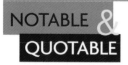

Spoiling your Yorkshire Terrier can result in a dog that makes himself the head of the house. When Yorkies own the house, a number of bad things can happen. The dog becomes so unmanageable that he ends up in a shelter.

— *Linda York, founder and president of Pet Pals Inc. of Goshen County, Wy.*

Marion Lane's Yorkie, "The Wee," was extremely intense in her job as unofficial floor monitor of their apartment building in Queens, N.Y. She was on duty 24/7. Lane had persuaded herself that because none of the neighbors had complained, they hadn't noticed or didn't mind The Wee's proprietary attitude about her floor.

One day in the elevator, Lane ran into one of her neighbors, a merchant marine bachelor whose tour of duty spanned from 4 p.m. to midnight. A German immigrant, the dour gentleman eyed her coldly for a few moments before saying, "Zat rotten dog of yours! She tells the whole building vat time I come in zu hause."

Fortunately, this neighbor's point of view was balanced by another's, who told Lane how happy she was that The Wee barked at every stranger on the floor. "I don't have to worry about strangers," she said. "Your dog knows who belongs here and who doesn't."

Yorkies also are intense in their relationships. They seem to either love the whole world, or relate to only one person, and rarely anything in between.

Lynn Hoover, the Pittsburgh-based founder of the International Association of Animal Behavior Consultants, thought that her Yorkie, Piper, was essentially a one-woman dog who was devoted to her owner and only mildly interested in other people. She tells the story of once leaving Piper with one of her daughter's friends, a young woman named Amy, while the family went on vacation.

While they were away, Amy let Piper sleep on her pillow. Four months later, Amy stopped by the house for a visit. "She was two floors down, and Piper started jumping up and down and scratching at the door—she was a dog in a hurry," Hoover says. "When I opened the door, she raced downstairs to the game room and jumped all over Amy, delighted to see her old friend. She remembered. For a Yorkie, love is forever."

SMART TIP!

If you know your little Napoleon will race up to larger dogs, make it a point to cross the street when you see one coming. Also, because some people allow their dogs to roam off-leash, be prepared to hoist your Yorkie out of harm's way. A harness instead of a collar is great for emergency pickups.

A TERRIER AT HEART

When the Yorkshire Terrier is given access to the great outdoors, however, he takes to it with zeal. He is a terrier, after all, and the word "terrier" derives from the Latin word for earth. Yorkies love to play in the grass—and dirt. Despite their small size, they are talented diggers. Yorkies enjoy competing in all the sporting games of the larger terriers. Although the Yorkie has neither the poundage of the Dandie Dinmont nor the legginess of the Airedale, some of the tenaciousness and pluck of his terrier ancestors still race through his blue arteries.

Most Yorkshire Terrier owners admit that being owned by a Yorkshire Terrier is

indoors, with an occasional romp through the yard. They are ideal for apartment dwellers or others living in small townhouses without much access to the outdoors.

Yorkies need to be taught to stay out from underfoot. While they're learning, don't lift your feet off the ground. Older people might consider wearing a bell, so the Yorkie knows they're coming. Children could do this, too. It's worth it to avoid stepping on the dog and possibly breaking his leg or foot.

—breeder Muriel Campanella of Woodside, N.Y.

Yorkies love to be spoiled, but you must resist the urge! This breed should be treated like dogs, not like prima donnas.

infectious. Yorkies are not just great family dogs, they are family! Owners consider their Yorkies to be a part of the family, like any other child in the household. Given the Yorkie's size and the giant size of his heart and character, it is no surprise that smart owners depend on their Yorkies for companionship and affection. Thus, many true Yorkshire Terrier fanciers build a whole family of Yorkies. While most dog breeders will discuss their kennel plans, it is rare to hear a Yorkie breeder talk about a "kennel." The Yorkshire is a home buddy, always living amid the family, totally immersed and involved in the family's day-to-day routine.

Yorkies operate on the family's schedule. They instinctively know who comes home first, and, likewise, they know when someone is late or missing. This family dog cannot sleep if one of his beloved is still not home where he or she belongs. While the Yorkie counts his master or mistress first (like all dogs, the one who feeds and cares for him receives special consideration), every member of the family is regarded in the highest esteem.

A word of caution to the overzealous Yorkie lover: You must resist your primal urge to spoil your Yorkshire Terrier beyond reason. Any overly pampered dog can become difficult to live with. Considering this toy terrier's spirit and determination, once a Yorkie thinks he has his way in all matters of the household, he may become less of a joy to have around. By nature, the

Yorkies may be on the smaller side, but their attitudes aren't!

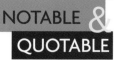

NOTABLE & QUOTABLE

Yorkie's can sometimes be just a little too big for their britches. They are independent at times and can be hard-headed.

—breeder Kathy Murphy, from Holbrook, Az.

As small as they are, Yorkies are determined climbers and jumpers. To protect your Yorkie from injury as he lands on hard or slippery surfaces, place nonslip rugs or carpeting around sofas, beds, and other favorite lookout points.

Yorkie is not a selfish, greedy dog; he is not a stingy eater and does not gorge himself; he does not hide his toys from his playmates and is quite happy to share his things. Once your obsession has spoiled this delightful personality, your Yorkie may not be the generous, open-hearted angel you fell in love with.

Be careful. Many Yorkie-a-holics have embarrassing stories about the extent to which they go to spoil their adorable little friends. Some Yorkie owners purchase cradles and high chairs for their Yorkies; visit the butcher daily to furnish top-grade sirloin; cancel vacation plans if the six Yorkies were not invited; and knit and crochet sweaters and hats for their dogs. If you find yourself falling into any of the those categories, then you will fit in well with the wonderfully dedicated, delicately balanced world of Yorkshire Terrier ownership.

It's difficult not to love a cuddly breed like the Yorkie!

When Harvey and Mildred Zenreich of East Elmhurst, N.Y., visited their neighbors to show off their Yorkie, Jane Ray Too, the antics began right away.

As soon as Jane's paws hit the sidewalk, she flew to the end of her leash and led her senior-citizen owners up the front steps and into the living room. Without missing a beat, Jane picked up the neighbor dogs' squeaky red plush bone and took possession of it. In the next minutes, she raced back and forth between this newfound treasure to the neighbors—virtual strangers to her—rocketing from one lap to the other and back again. She was a silver-and-tan dervish: up on the sofa, down again, into the dining room to bark at the neighbors' rabbit, Hildegard, then back again to reclaim the red bone or leap onto one of their laps.

Mildred and Harvey stayed for ninety minutes. While they drank tea and talked, Jane Ray Too, named after Mildred's favorite pattern of Depression glass—the second of her Yorkies to receive this name—never settled down.

She relinquished the red bone in favor of the cat's purple tinsel ball. This she brought to everyone in turn. What Jane clearly wanted was for someone (anyone!) to toss it for her to retrieve—again, and again, and again.

Eventually, she dropped the ball to climb to the top of the sofa, which gave her a vantage point above the rabbit's enclosure. Anyone could see she was considering the pros and cons of jumping down into the enclosure with Hildegard. Her vigil was broken only when Mildred asked, "Jane, do you want to go in the car?" Those magic words brought Jane bouncing to the floor and heading straight to the front door. Without a backward glance, she was on to the next adventure. Typical Yorkie!

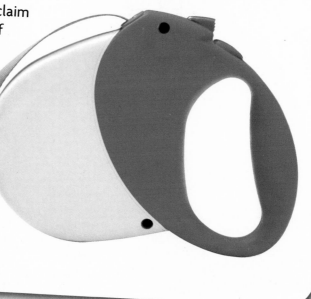

YORKSHIRE TERRIER TEMPLATE

This spirited, spunky terrier offers a big personality in a small package.

COUNTRY OF ORIGIN: England

WHAT HIS FRIENDS CALL HIM: Yorkie

SIZE: 4 to 7 pounds

COAT & COLOR: coat is glossy, fine, and silky in texture. Coat is moderately long and perfectly straight; blue (black) and tan in color.

PERSONALITY TRAITS: intelligent, courageous, and affectionate. The brave Yorkie originally was bred to catch rats in clothing mills, and his fearlessness and energy have not diminished with time. Yorkshire Terriers are consistently one of the most popular breeds in the United States, and with their fun, adventurous nature, it is easy to see why people love Yorkies so much!

WITH KIDS: recommended for adults and older, considerate children; best with an only child

WITH OTHER PETS: Yorkshire Terriers are even-tempered and live well with other pets.

ENERGY LEVEL: very high

EXERCISE NEEDS: Daily walks are a must, as are regular play sessions and lots of interaction with their owners.

GROOMING NEEDS: requires daily brushing and combing

TRAINING NEEDS: Yorkies are intelligent and easy to train, but can become demanding and may nip if spoiled.

LIVING ENVIRONMENT: Yorkies are adaptable and because of their small size and good nature, they live well in an apartment or in a home, in a city or in the country.

LIFESPAN: 12 to 15 years

While the Industrial Revolution led most of the world toward pursuing the bigger and better, some brilliant engineers sought smaller and better. The Yorkshire Terrier is a remarkable manmade creation of the mid-19th century, a time when British dog enthusiasts were crossing many types of terriers in order to develop dogs who were handsomely suited for their needs.

In Yorkshire and Lancashire counties, the breed we now know as the Yorkshire Terrier emerged in his most recognizable form. The first shows for toy terriers in Great Britain began in 1860, and "Yorkshires" from these two textile counties were counted among the first ribbon holders.

TINY TERRIER ORIGINS

Britons needed small terriers. Back in the 11th century, farmers and serfs couldn't own large dogs because wealthy landowners wanted to discourage poaching on their property. One story says that peasant-class dogs in Britain had to be able to fit through

Did You Know? In the late 1800s, as dog shows became more popular, more people began exhibiting Yorkshire Terriers as show dogs and keeping them as pets. Although Yorkies were probably still used as ratters, their appearance became more important during this time and breeders began to improve the coat and standardize the breed's size and shape.

a seven-inch hoop. Then, reasoned the landowners, they couldn't do too much damage as poachers. Little did they know how feisty these small terriers could be, helping corner and dispatch rabbits, squirrels, and other small game with a speedy chase, a targeted attack, and sharp barks to signal that the varmint had been cornered. These little dogs played an important role in helping to nourish their human families because rabbits and other small game poached from the property of the wealthy landowners meant dinner on the table. Should the landowner approach, a small terrier could also easily hide, or leap out of sight into the farmer's pack.

Because they had long coats, these terriers were easier to grab and scoop into packs for hiding, or to pull from a rodent burrow. Their dark body coloration helped camouflage them, but the lighter head helped their owners spot them for easier retrieval from a rabbit hole. Even today, a Yorkie will still go to ground, burrowing or following a critter into its hole. On a Yorkie's turf, no small critter is safe from the chase.

Small terriers also served an important role as an all-purpose helper. They would kill rats and vermin in the farmer's fields, and they would chase rabbits out of the vegetable gardens.

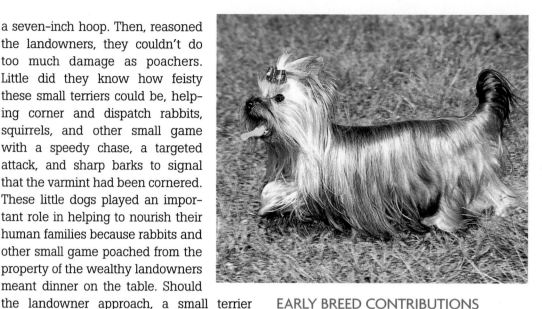

EARLY BREED CONTRIBUTIONS

Which breeds contributed to the composition of the Yorkshire Terrier, however, is still a great debate. Among the contenders are the Toy Manchester Terrier, Maltese, Skye Terrier, Dandie Dinmont Terrier, and two extinct breeds known as the Paisley Terrier and the Clydesdale Terrier. The Paisley is described as smaller than the Skye and shorter in back, with gray coloration and a rougher coat. The Clydesdale also bore resemblance to the Skye of today, with the characteristic well-feathered prick ears, a floor-length coat in dark blue with tan markings on the face, legs and feet, and a long body.

The Clydesdale, Paisley, and Skye terriers receive credit for the Yorkshire Terrier's length of coat; the Maltese for coat and the diminu-

Did You Know?

The Yorkie's coat should be glossy, fine, and silky in texture. Coat on the body is moderately long and straight, not wavy. The fall on the head is long and tied with one bow in the center or parted in the middle and tied with two bows. The muzzle hair is long, but hair on the tips of the ears should be trimmed short. In addition, the feet can be trimmed to give them a neat appearance.

NOTABLE & QUOTABLE

I call Yorkies "the Sir Lancelots of dogdom." They are marvelous companions with so much energy. They may be bred down to toy size, but they are always a terrier first.

—Shirley Patterson, Yorkshire Terrier Club of America member from Pottstown, Pa.

tive size; and the Manchester for coloration. The silken texture of the Yorkie's coat could have come from all of the longer-coated dogs in the mixture, even though the Paisley and Clydesdale were usually rough-coated. Whenever silky-coated puppies occurred in a Paisley or Clydesdale litter, they were discarded until a fad for silky coats emerged. Both of these rough-coated terriers lost favor, and their numbers began to diminish.

The smaller Manchester Terriers that were incorporated into the early stock were fierce ratters, working side by side with miners, killing off the vermin, with neither fear nor sympathy toward their prey. These dogs killed rats not only for employment, but also for entertainment. Toward the end of the 19th century, rat-killing contests became very popular. The small black and tan terriers, with their smooth coats and fiery temperaments, proved very adept at the quick-fire killing of their ratine foes. Judged against the clock, the dogs had to kill as many rats as possible in a given time frame. Some dogs were able to slay a couple hundred rats in a mere ten-minute timeframe!

SCOTTISH ROOTS, ENGLISH BRANCHES

The Industrial Revolution (18th and 19th centuries) changed Europe's face, and nowhere more than in Great Britain. As machines began to replace human laborers, people were forced to move from their isolated homes and towns to find work. One such movement brought an influx of people from Scotland to Yorkshire, England, where numerous mines and mills needed laborers. Just as we would bring our dogs with us today if we moved, so did these Scots, many of whom were weavers.

History gives us many examples of professions that gravitated toward certain dog breeds, and the Scottish weavers had a fondness for long-coated, small terriers, perhaps because their beautiful coats suggested the very fabrics they created. The small Scottish terriers included the Skye, Clydesdale, and Paisley terriers, which ranged from eight to more than twenty pounds. These terriers all had short legs, long backs, and long, harsh coats. One legend says that the weavers handling wool all day often had lanolin all over their hands, so they used their small terriers as hand towels. This would be a handy way to remove the grease from working human hands, and at the same time, condition the long terrier coat.

it's a Fact

The Yorkie's tail is docked to a medium length and is carried slightly higher than the back.

Small terriers were perfect companions for weavers and other tradesmen because they kept vermin out of the shops, warehouses and homes. Another story surmises that people kept their terriers in the bottom cupboards, where vermin were likely to hide. This early form of the kennel may have been an ideal situation for everyone. The terriers had a safe place to rest with the occasional excitement of something small and furry to chase.

A popular form of entertainment at the time was to test a terrier's ratting ability. Terriers had to catch as many rats as the number of pounds they weighed, and whichever terrier could do this fastest was proclaimed the winner. For this reason, people bred their terriers to be fierce and small. A four-pound terrier only had to catch four rats before its twelve-pound rival caught a dozen rats, so this further encouraged breeders to reduce the Yorkshire Terrier's size.

With this concentrated population of small terriers, it was only a matter of time before a unique local breed emerged from the blending of the terriers newly congregated in Yorkshire. Scottish terriers may have mixed with local terriers, such as the Waterside Terrier, a short-legged terrier that roamed the rivers and canals, living on rats, toward the end of the 18th century in Yorkshire. As the dogs mixed and various mutations occurred—the occasional smaller or larger dog, the occasional silkier or longer coat—people began to call this new local dog by various names. Sometimes called the Broken Haired Scotch Terrier or simply Scotch Terrier, the breed finally earned its own name in 1870.

A reporter named Angus Sutherland wrote for a British magazine, *The Field,* about the new little terrier becoming so popular in Yorkshire, which was descended from the terriers of Scotland: "They ought no

Yorkies are perfect lap dogs because they are small, love attention and are loyal to their owners.

No one knew how she'd landed in a New Guinea foxhole—but when the soldier found the little Yorkie in February 1944, her life was changed forever.

Her name was Smoky, and she was starving. The soldier who found her fed her, but when he needed money to stay in a poker game, he sold Smoky for two Australian pounds to Corp. Bill Wynne. That was when Smoky began to show that she was as tough as any other war dog, large or small.

For the rest of World War II, Smoky served with Wynne and the rest of the Fifth Air Force, 26th Photo Reconnaissance Squadron. She endured the same living conditions that the rest of the squadron did: sleeping in a tent, sharing food, surviving air raids, and living through a typhoon on Okinawa. During down times, Wynne trained the little Yorkie to perform tricks to entertain the troops, as well as wounded soldiers in military hospitals. Smoky also went with Wynne on more than 150 air raids and several air-sea rescue missions. Amazingly, she jumped from a thirty-foot tower, wearing a parachute designed especially for her!

Her best-known feat capitalized on her breed's ability to get in and out of tight spots. Engineers who were building an airfield for Allied war planes needed to run a telegraph wire through a seventy-foot underground pipe that was only 8 inches in diameter. To make matters worse, soil had spilled through the pipe's joints, reducing the diameter to only 4 inches. The Signal Corps, which needed the wire, asked Wynne whether Smoky could run the wire from one end of the pipe to the other. Wynne agreed to let her try, and Smoky became an instant hero.

Smoky also capitalized on her breed's reputation for protectiveness during an airborne attack on the U.S. transport ship that she and Wynne were traveling on. While the ship deck boomed and vibrated from the ship's anti-aircraft fire, Smoky warned Wynne of an incoming shell. According to Wynne, Smoky prompted him to duck the shellfire that hit the eight men standing next to them.

After the war, Wynne took Smoky home to Cleveland, Ohio. For the next decade, the two performed in Hollywood and elsewhere, as well as at veterans' hospitals. She died in 1957 at approximately fourteen years of age. Today, Cleveland boasts two monuments to Smoky: one in the Eastlake Doggie Park (www.clevelanddogparks.com) and one in the Cleveland Metroparks Rocky River Reservation (www.clemetparks.com).

longer to be called Scotch Terriers, but Yorkshire Terriers, for having so improved there," Sutherland wrote.

Because terriers at this time were bred for working and not for show, they varied a lot in size and coat type. Some dogs exceeded eighteen pounds, but others barely reached five pounds. Some coats were rougher and wirier; others were smoother and silkier. According to Joan Gordon of Glenview, Ill., a charter member of the YTCA who has bred Yorkshire Terriers since 1948, the two breeds were finally separated for show purposes into two groups according to size. The larger became Broken Haired Scotch Terriers and the smaller became Yorkshire Terriers. "About half the dogs in both groups were actually sired by the same dog, Huddersfield Ben," Gordon says.

HUDDERSFIELD BEN

In 1865, a dog was born who became the father of the Yorkshire Terrier breed as we know it today. An influential sire and dog-show winner, his name was Huddersfield Ben. He lived only six years, suffering an untimely death when he ran across a road and was struck by a carriage, but in those six short years, he had an unprecedented impact on the breed that would follow in his little paw prints. Mrs. M.A. Foster owned Huddersfield Ben. She was one of the best-known Yorkie breeders at the time, and also the first woman ever to judge a dog show in England.

Huddersfield Ben and the York-shire Terrier breed as a whole descended from just three dogs, according to an 1887 article in *The English Stockkeeper* news-paper, written by E. Bootman from Halifax, Yorkshire. These progenitors of the Yorkshire Terrier were hardly from any long lines of aristo-cratic terriers, but from crossbred terri-ers who did not have pedigrees.

The first was a mixed Scotch Terrier named Swift's Old Crab, owned by a carpenter in Halifax.

Crab weighed about nine pounds, had a long body, tan legs and muzzle, and a coat of about 3 or 4 inches. The next was a female named Kershaw's Kitty, a Skye Terrier who had been stolen from Manchester and sent to a saddlemaker in Huddersfield, who then sent her to a waiter at the White Swan Hotel in Halifax for hiding when he found out a reward was posted for her return. From there, J. Kershaw of Bishop Blaise, who owned a public house in Halifax, adopted "Kitty."

Kitty had six litters totaling thirty-six puppies with Crab as the father, and these two terriers were largely responsible for stocking the general area with small terriers. When Kitty was then given to F. Jagger in 1851, she had forty-four more puppies. She was quite a busy mother, logging eighty puppies total. She had drop ears and a long blue coat with no tan markings.

The final Yorkshire Terrier progenitor was an Old English Terrier (a now-extinct breed) with a tan head, ears, and legs, and a grizzled back. This dog's name has been lost to history. She belonged to Bernard Harltey of Allen Gate in Halifax, and was sent to him by a friend living in Scotland. He later gave her to his coachman, who gave her to a friend named Whittam. She also produced many puppies, and although she was sent from Scotland, records suggest her parents were probably also from Halifax.

The puppies resulting from these three prolific terriers—all natives or near-natives of Yorkshire—continued to evolve according to the fancies of their owners and breeders. In

the late 1800s, as dog shows became more popular, more people began exhibiting Yorkshire Terriers as show dogs and keep them as pets. Although Yorkies probably were still used as ratters, their appearance became more important during this time and breeders began to improve the coat and standardize the breed's size and shape. The Yorkshire Terrier became a toy terrier, charming all those who met it while still retaining its fiery terrier spirit.

The Yorkshire Terrier was among the first breeds recognized by the newly formed Kennel Club in 1873. A quarter century passed, however, before the breed's official

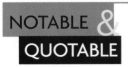

NOTABLE & QUOTABLE

Not everyone can understand the "I-am-in-control" attitude of a Yorkshire Terrier. He was originally a ratter and that "kill-the-varmint" attitude is still inside his beautiful little body.

—Yorkshire Terrier breeder Linda Grimm of Valrico, Fla.

standard was drafted. Established in 1898, England's Yorkshire Terrier Club formed in order to write a standard for the breed.

YORKIES IN THE UNITED STATES

The first blue and tan to be heralded in the land of the red, white, and blue was Belle, a female whelped in 1877, owned by A. E. Godeffroy. Belle was registered before the American Kennel Club was formed, in a ledger belonging to A. N. Rouse. Two other early imports, among the first in the AKC Stud Book, were known as Jim and Rose, both derived from Scottish breeding. They were owned by J. A. Nickerson and R. R. Bushell of Boston, Mass.

Around 1900, George Stedman Thomas, imported four of the original Yorkshire Terriers to the States, and joined forces with Charles N. Symonds to promote the breed. Thomas is credited with championing the Yorkie in the breed ring, and he exhibited his dogs at Westminster Kennel Club for more than twenty-five years. He and his wife won many blue ribbons during this period and really put the little Yorkie on the show-dog map in the United States.

The 1930s was marked by many significant wins for Yorkies in the ring. The year 1933 began a remarkable trend for the breed at the Westminster Show. Earl Byng placed fourth in the Group at Westminster, and, in 1934, Ch. Haslingden Dandy Dinty placed third. Both of these dogs were owned by Andrew Patterson. For the next three years, Yorkies placed in the Group: Ch. Rochdale

Queen of the Toys, owned by John Shipp, in 1935; and Ch. Bobbie B. III, owned by Samuel Baxter, in 1936 and 1937. After a string of impressive wins, finally in 1939, a Yorkie won the Group: Ch. Miss Wynsum, owned by Arthur Mills, the owner of the Millbarry Kennels, easily the most prominent Yorkie breeders of the 1930s. Many decades would pass before a Yorkie would win Best in Show at Westminster, however.

The breed rose in popularity in the 1940s, and by the 1950s, there were more American breeders than ever. In 1951, the Yorkshire Terrier Club of America was founded, when a group of ten influential

Yorkie fanciers from around the country met at the California home of Kay Finch. The following year, the club held its first sanctioned match in Los Angeles, with more than fifty Yorkshire Terriers entered. The club was accepted by the AKC in 1958 and the breed standard, based largely on the British standard, was accepted by 1966. That standard has remained in effect, with minor changes, until the present day. The club has grown to include over 500 members with more than twenty regional clubs around the country. The Yorkie Express, a quarterly newsletter, is distributed by the club.

The Yorkie's stronghold in the States began to firm up in the 1950s and the following decades, and the legions of breeders are too many to name here. It goes without saying that the Yorkshire Terrier in the United States, through the efforts of the parent club and thousands of breeders, exhibitors, and judges, has become the nation's number-one toy breed. The AKC registers around 40,000 Yorkie puppies each year out of about 25,000 litters! The quality of the breed in the States continues to be high and the breed is in the competent hands of the many responsible fanciers who devote their worlds to the irresistible Yorkshire Terrier.

it's a Fact

In L. Frank Baum's book, *The Wonderful Wizard of Oz*, Toto is described as "a little black dog with long silky hair." That sounds more like a Yorkshire Terrier than the Cairn Terrier, who played the role in the 1939 film version.

Smart owners should set out to purchase the best Yorkshire Terrier that they can possibly afford. The safest method of obtaining your puppy is to seek out a local reputable breeder. This is suggested even if you are not looking for a show-quality dog. Novice breeders and pet owners who advertise at attractive prices in the local newspapers are probably kind enough toward their dogs, but perhaps do not have the expertise or facilities required to successfully raise these animals. These pet puppies are frequently badly weaned and left with their mother too long without any supplemental feeding. This lack of proper feeding can cause indigestion, rickets, weak bones, poor teeth, and other problems. Veterinary bills may soon distort initial savings into financial or, worse, emotional loss.

You want to find an established breeder, someone who's been breeding Yorkies for at least ten years and who belongs to his local and national breed clubs. Such a breeder has demonstrated outstanding dog ethics and a strong commitment to the Yorkie breed. An established breeder will be happy to answer your questions and make you comfortable with your choice of the Yorkshire Terrier, even being able to explain

it's a Fact The Yorkshire Terrier Club of America code of ethics requires breeder members to keep their puppies for twelve weeks, before sending them to their forever homes.

Be sure to meet the puppy's mother and father, if possible. They will give you a clue as to what your pup will look and act like in the future.

the subtle differences in temperament and behavior between individual dogs. A good breeder will sell you a puppy at a fair price if, and only if, he determines that you are a suitable, worthy owner of his dogs. The breeder can be relied upon for advice, no matter what time of day or night, and will accept a puppy back, without questions, should you decide that this is not the right dog for you.

When choosing a breeder, reputation and qualifications are much more important than where the breeder is located. A three- or four-hour drive to pick up a new family member should not be considered inconvenience.

Choosing a breeder is an important first step in dog ownership. Fortunately, most Yorkie breeders are devoted to the breed and its well-being, though be aware that there are backyard Yorkshire Terrier "breeders" who take advantage of the breed's popularity and the ignorance of many new dog purchasers. With a little research and knowledge, potential owners should have little problem finding a reputable Yorkie breeder who doesn't live too far away. Start with your local all-breed kennel club or Yorkshire Terrier club. The American Kennel Club can direct you to the club or clubs nearest you; visit them online at www.akc.org. The Yorkie

it's a Fact

On average, a female Yorkshire Terrier only whelps between one and four puppies per litter.

Club of America maintains a breeder-referral service and also can put you in touch with your local club. The YTCA can be found online at www.ytca.org

Referrals are an excellent way to find a puppy. If you see a Yorkie you like, find out where he came from. Ask about any health problems and the dog's temperament. Also ask if the breeder was easy to work with. If that breeder doesn't have a puppy for you, he may be able to refer you to someone with similar lines.

Potential owners are encouraged to attend dog shows, obedience trails, or some other kind of performance event to see Yorkies in action, to meet the owners and handlers firsthand, and to get an idea of what Yorkies look like outside a photographer's studio. New owners may be surprised to see how large a Yorkie male is, or how small a female is. There's nothing like seeing Yorkshire Terriers live and up close. Provided you approach the handlers or owners at dog shows when they are not terribly busy, most are more than willing to answer questions, recommend breeders and give advice. Yorkshire Terrier people love to talk about their favorite topic: Yorkies!

MEET AND GREET

Now it's time to meet one or two breeders and their dogs. If the breeder has young puppies, he may not allow you to visit for a few weeks to ensure their safety. Whether he has puppies when you visit or not, never go from one kennel to another without going home, showering, and changing clothes, including your shoes (or clean them thoroughly, and spray the bottoms and sides with a ten-percent bleach solution). It is extremely easy to transmit deadly, infectious disease and parasites from one kennel to another, even if everything looks clean.

Meet as many of your potential puppy's relatives as possible. You should be able to meet the mother unless the puppies are very young. Don't expect her to look her best while she's nursing—puppy care is a big job for canine moms. Pay attention to her temperament. It is normal for a female dog to be protective of her babies, but she should accept your presence if her owner vouches for you. If the sire (father) is on the property, ask to meet him. He may not be present, because serious breeders often breed their females to stud dogs owned by other people. You should be able to see pictures of him, though. If you don't like the parents—either the body type or temperament—don't buy the puppy. Pups tend to look and act like their parents.

Take a look around. Does the environment look and smell reasonably clean? Do all the dogs appear to be healthy, with clear eyes, trimmed toenails, and well-groomed coats?

Look beyond the cute factor and choose a puppy who meshes well with your lifestyle and life needs.

Do they have fresh water to drink and room to move and play? Are they friendly? Does the breeder know every dog by name and each puppy as an individual? If the answer to any of these questions is no, look elsewhere. If the answers are yes, though, and you feel comfortable

with this breeder and like his dogs, and he feels comfortable with you, you may soon be owned by a Yorkie puppy.

SELECTING A PUPPY

Once you have contacted and met a breeder or two and made your choice about which breeder is best suited to your needs, it's time to visit the litter. Keep in mind that many top breeders have waiting lists. Sometimes new owners have to wait as long as two years for a puppy. If you are really committed to the breeder you've selected, then you will wait (and hope for an early arrival!). If not, you may have to resort to your second- or third-choice breeder. Don't be too anxious, however. If the breeder doesn't have anyone interested in his puppies, there is probably a good reason.

Because breeding Yorkies is a very delicate matter, and breeders must always test their breeding stock before producing a litter, most breeders do not expect a litter every season, or, for that matter, even every year. Patience is a virtue for a Yorkie owner.

You are likely to be choosing a Yorkie as a pet dog and not as a show dog, so select a pup who is friendly and attractive. Yorkies generally have relatively small litters, averaging five puppies, so selection is limited once you have located a desirable litter. Beware of the shy or overly aggressive puppy; be especially conscious of the nervous Yorkie pup. Don't let sentiment or emotion trap you into buying the runt of the litter. Keep health and sound breeding foremost in your selection.

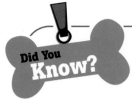

Did You Know?

Signs of a Good Breeder
When you visit a breeder, be on the lookout for:
- a clean, well-maintained facility
- no overwhelming odors
- overall impression of cleanliness
- socialized dogs and puppies

Breeders commonly allow visitors to see the litter by around the fifth or sixth week, and puppies leave for their new homes between the eighth and tenth week. Breeders who permit their puppies to leave earlier are more interested in your money than in their puppies' well-being.

Puppies need to learn the rules of the trade from their moms, and most mothers continue teaching the pups manners and dos and don'ts until around the eighth week. Breeders spend significant amounts of time with the

JOIN OUR ONLINE
Club Yorkie®

Questions to Expect
Be prepared for the breeder to ask you some questions, too.

some breeders only insist on meeting the children first to see how they handle puppies. It all depends on the breeder.

1. Have you previously owned a Yorkshire Terrier?
The breeder is trying to gauge how familiar you are with the breed. If you have never owned one, illustrate your knowledge of Yorkies by telling the breeder about your research.

2. Do you have children? What ages?
Some breeders are wary about selling a small dog to families with younger children. This isn't a steadfast rule, and

3. How long have you wanted a Yorkshire Terrier?
This helps a breeder know if this purchase is an impulse buy, or a carefully thought-out decision. Buying on impulse is one of the biggest mistakes owners can make. Be patient.

Join Club Yorkie to get a complete list of questions a breeder should ask you. Click on "downloads" at:
DogChannel.com/Club-Yorkie

Good breeders care about who they sell their pups to. They're not just out to make a quick buck.

Yorkie toddlers so that they are able to interact with humans.

Given the long history between dogs and humans, bonding between the two species is natural but must be nurtured. A well-bred, well-socialized Yorkshire Terrier puppy wants nothing more than to be near you and to please you.

ESSENTIAL PAPERWORK

Make sure the breeder has proper papers to go with the puppy of your choice.

Contract: You should receive a copy of the purchase contract you signed when you bought your puppy. The contract should specify the purchase price, health guarantee, spay/neuter requirements by a certain age, and conditions to return the pup if you find that you can't keep him for any reason.

Registration Papers: If the breeder said that the puppy's parents were registered with the American Kennel Club or United Kennel Club, you should receive an application form to register your puppy—or at the very least, a signed bill of sale that you can use to register the puppy. The bill of sale should include the puppy's breed, date of birth, sex, registered names of the parents,

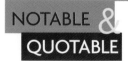

NOTABLE & QUOTABLE

Good temperament is one of the qualities reputable breeders always breed for. They also spend a lot of time and energy socializing the puppies.

—Robert Owen, Yorkie breeder from Elizabethtown, Ky.

Are you looking for a pet who will worship the ground you walk on?

Rescue volunteers suggest that people peel their eyes away from those appealing, tempting puppies and consider adopting an older Yorkie who's four, five, or six years old or even older.

Sometimes, a Yorkshire Terrier finds himself without a home. Perhaps his owner decides he can't or won't put in the time needed to care for the dog or can't figure out how to train him. Such a dog may be surrendered to a Yorkie rescue group, which then works to find him a new and hopefully permanent home.

These groups sometimes have young puppies available for adoption, and often have older puppies or adolescents. To find a Yorkie rescue group, log onto the Yorkshire Terrier Club of America website, www.ytca.org, for more information.

There are plenty of benefits to adopting a rescued Yorkshire Terrier. Such dogs have passed the chewing stage, have learned basic bathroom manners—and still have many years left. In addition, many rescue volunteers believe that the older dog realizes he's been saved, and repays his savior by showing lots of love and devotion.

Another way to find a Yorkie puppy or adult who needs a new home is to log onto a national pet adoption website such as Petfinder.com (www.petfinder.com). The site's searchable database enables you to find a Yorkshire Terrier in your area who needs a break in the form of a compassionate owner like you.

litter number, the breeder's name, date of sale, and the seller's signature. Registration allows your puppy to compete in kennel club–sanctioned events such as agility, obedience, and rally events. Registration fees support research and other activities sponsored by the organization. If your intention is to show your Yorkie, be sure not to purchase a puppy that the breeder promises is "AKC registration eligible" because it's unlikely he will be; only fully registered dogs can participate in AKC conformation shows.

Pedigree: The breeder should include a copy of your puppy's family tree, listing your puppy's parents, grandparents, great-grandparents, and beyond, depending on how many generations the pedigree includes. It also lists any degrees and/or

Breeder Q&A

Here are some questions you should ask a breeder and the preferred answers you want.

Q. How often do you have litters available?

A. The answer you want to hear is "once or twice a year" or "occasionally" because a breeder who doesn't have litters all that often is probably more concerned with the quality of his puppies, rather than with producing a lot of puppies to make money.

Q. What is the goal of your breeding program?

A. A good answer is "to improve the breed" or "to breed for temperament."

Q. When do your pups go to their homes?

A. Eight weeks or more is the right answer.

Q. What kinds of health problems have you had with your Yorkies?

A. Beware of a breeder who says, "none." Every breed has health issues. For terriers, some health problems include portosystemic (liver) shunt, retinal dysplasia, breathing problems and patellar luxation (dislocated kneecaps).

Get a complete list of questions to ask a Yorkie breeder—and the correct answers—on Club Yorkie. Log onto **DogChannel.com/Club-Yorkie** and click on "downloads."

Reputable breeders allow their pups to be adopted at a minimum of eight weeks of age.

titles that those relatives have earned. Look for indications that the dog's ancestors were active, successful achievers in various areas of the dog sport. The information that a pedigree provides can help you understand more about the physical conformation and/or behavioral accomplishments of your puppy's family. Usually the quality of the pedigree dictates the price of the puppy, so expect to pay a higher price for a higher quality puppy. However, chances are that you will be rewarded by the qual-

Did You Know?

Titles from dog sports, such as obedience and agility, are signs that a breeder is involved in competitive, fun activities with his dogs. Sometimes, those who are heavily involved in conformation simply don't have time to "do it all." These titles are definitely a plus, but they aren't necessary to prove a Yorkie's total worth.

Don't buy from breeders who advertise their pups as "teacups" or other sizes that aren't standard.

ity of life that you and your pedigreed Yorkie will enjoy!

Health Records: You should receive a copy of your puppy's health records, including his date of birth, visits to the vet, and immunizations. Bring the health records to your vet when you take your Yorkie puppy in for his first checkup, which should take place within a few days of his arrival in your household. The records will become part of your puppy's permanent health file.

Care Instructions: Finally, the breeder should provide written instructions on basic puppy care, including when and how much to feed him.

BUYER BEWARE

There's no such thing as a miniature Yorkie, tiny toy, teacup, or any other word that indicates a Yorkie weighing less than four pounds. A Yorkshire Terrier is a Yorkshire Terrier. The preferred weight range for this breed, according to the breed standard, is seven pounds or less—with reputable breeders trying to remain in the four- to seven-pound range for health reasons.

Did You Know?

If you purchase a Yorkie who is not eligible for American Kennel Club registration, your dog still may be able to participate in companion and performance events. The Purebred Alternative Listing Program/Indefinite Listing Privilege allows unregistered Yorkshire Terriers to enter agility trials, junior showmanship at dog shows, and obedience and rally trials. Visit the AKC's website (www.akc.org) for an application.

As with any breed of dog, a litter occasionally will have puppies that are below or above the breed's desired size range. Overly big Yorkies can make great pets; however, their size is a serious fault in the show ring. Extremely tiny Yorkies generally aren't shown because quality breeders feel the more miniscule the Yorkie, the higher the risk of health problems that can be passed along in their breeding programs.

There also are no rare colors in the Yorkshire Terrier. Again, the Yorkshire Terrier breed standard is very specific in the acceptable color ranges of the Yorkie's dark steel-blue and tan coat. Yes, there are Yorkies with black–and–tan or burgundy coats. There are Yorkies with silver–blue and tan coats. There are even Yorkies with blue coats pointed (intermingled) with bronze, fawn, or black hairs. Others are advertised as rare red or gold Yorkies, even those that are white, black, and tan in color. Though these coat colors do look unique, they don't make the dog more valuable.

Make sure you like your breeder because you'll probably return in a year or so for a second Yorkie!

Any deviation from the breed standard actually makes the Yorkie less valuable—a pet-quality pup (one that has minor cosmetic flaws that prevent it from competing in conformation). And, often extremely unusual coloring can indicate that the puppy is actually a mix of breeds rather than a true purebred Yorkshire Terrier.

Signs of a Healthy Puppy

Here are a few things you should look for when selecting a puppy from a litter.

1. **NOSE:** It should be slightly moist to the touch, but there shouldn't be excessive discharge. The puppy should not be sneezing or sniffling persistently.

2. **SKIN AND COAT:** The puppy's coat should be soft and shiny, without flakes or excessive shedding. Watch out for patches of missing hair, redness, bumps, or sores. The pup should have a pleasant smell. Check for parasites, such as fleas or ticks.

3. **BEHAVIOR:** A healthy puppy may be sleepy, but should not be lethargic. He will be playful at times, not isolated in a corner. You should see occasional bursts of energy and interaction with littermates. When it's mealtime, a healthy pup will take an interest in his food.

There are more signs to look for when picking out the perfect Yorkie puppy for you. Download the list at **DogChannel.com/Club-Yorkie**

A healthy puppy should have clear eyes, a moist nose and an interest in people and food.

ESSENTIALS

Yorkshire Terrier puppies are tiny, fragile, and vulnerable, but this doesn't make them any less interested in living the puppy life. They're going to want to run, jump, and play like any other dog breed. Is it possible to let your Yorkie enjoy being a dog without risking life and limb? Their natural curiosity can border on recklessness (they are terriers, you know!), which means that you'll need to puppy-proof your humble abode from the ground up.

How you prepare your home will depend on how much freedom your dog will be allowed. In the case of your Yorkie, designating a couple of rooms (without stairs) for a puppy is ideal.

In order for a puppy to grow into a stable, well-adjusted dog, he has to feel comfortable in his surroundings. Remember, he is leaving the warmth and security of his mother and littermates, as well as the familiarity of the only place he has ever known, so it is important to make his transition to your home—his *new* home—as easy as possible.

it's a **Fact**

Dangers lurk indoors and out. Keep your curious Yorkie from investigating your shed and garage. Antifreeze and fertilizers, such as those you would use for roses, will kill a Yorkshire Terrier. Keep these items on high shelves that are out of reach for your low-sniffing terrier.

PUPPY-PROOFING

Aside from making sure that your Yorkshire Terrier will be comfortable in your home, you also have to make sure that your home is safe, which means taking the proper precautions to keep your pup away from things that are dangerous for him.

Puppy-proof your home inside and out. Place breakables out of reach. If he is limited to certain places within the house, keep potentially dangerous items in off-limit areas. If your terrier is going to spend time in a crate, make sure that there is nothing near it that he can reach if he sticks his curious little nose or paws through the openings.

The outside of your home must also be safe for your pup. Your puppy will naturally want to run and explore the yard, and he should be granted that freedom—as long as

you are there to supervise him. Do not let a fence give you a false sense of security; you would be surprised how crafty (and persistent) a dog can be in figuring out how to dig under a fence or squeeze his way through

small holes. And because of his small size, your Yorkie can slip through the tiniest of holes. The remedy is to make the fence well embedded into the ground. Be sure to repair or secure any gaps in the fence. Check the fence periodically to ensure that it is in good shape and make repairs as needed; a very determined pup may work on the same spot until he is able to get through.

The following are a few common problem areas to watch out for in the home.

■ **Electrical cords and wiring:** No electrical cord or wiring is safe. Many office-supply stores sell products to keep wires gathered under computer desks, as well as products that prevent office chair wheels (and puppy teeth) from damaging electrical cords. If you have exposed cords and wires, these products aren't very expensive and can be used to keep a pup out of trouble.

■ **Trash cans:** Don't waste your time trying to train your Yorkie not to get into the trash. Simply put the garbage behind a cabinet door and use a child-safe lock if necessary. Dogs love bathroom trash (i.e., cotton balls, cotton swabs, used razors, dental floss, etc.), which consists of items that are all extremely dangerous! Put this trash can in a cabinet under the sink and make sure you always shut the door to the bathroom.

Protect your precious pooch by removing all potential hazards from his living area.

■ **Household cleaners:** Make sure your Yorkie puppy doesn't have access to any of these deadly chemicals. Keep them behind closed cabinet doors, using child-safe locks if necessary.

■ **Pest control sprays and poisons:** Chemicals to control ants or other pests should never be used in the house, if possible. Your pup doesn't have to directly ingest these poisons to become ill; if the Yorkie steps in the poison, he can experience toxic effects by licking his paws. Roach motels and other poisonous pest traps are also evidently yummy to dogs, so don't drop these poisons behind couches or cabinets; if there's room for a roach motel, there's room for a determined Yorkshire Terrier.

■ **Fabric:** Here's one you might not think about: Some puppies have a habit of licking blankets, upholstery, rugs, or carpets. Though this habit seems fairly innocuous, over time the fibers from the upholstery or carpet can accumulate in the dog's stomach and cause a blockage. If you see your dog licking these items, remove the item or prevent him from having contact with it.

■ **Prescriptions, painkillers, supplements, and vitamins:** Keep all medications in a cabinet. Also, be very careful when taking your prescription medications, supplements or vitamins: How often have you dropped a pill? With a Yorkshire Terrier, you can be assured that your puppy will be in between your legs and will snarf up the pill before you can even start to say "No!" Dispense your own pills carefully and without your Yorkie present.

■ **Miscellaneous loose items:** If it's not bolted to the floor, your puppy is likely to give the item a taste test. Socks, coins, children's toys, game pieces, cat bell balls—you name it; if it's on the floor, it's worth a try. Make sure the floors in your home are picked up and free of clutter.

FAMILY INTRODUCTIONS

Everyone in the house will be excited about the puppy's homecoming and will want to pet and play with him, but it is best to make the introduction low-key so as not to overwhelm the puppy. He already will be apprehensive. It is the first time he has been separated from his mother, littermates, and the breeder, and the ride to your home is

JOIN OUR ONLINE Club Yorkie®

Before you bring your Yorkshire Terrier home, make sure you don't have anything that can put him in harm's way. Go to Club Yorkie and download a list of poisonous plants and foods to avoid. Log on to **DogChannel.com/Club-Yorkie** and click on "downloads."

NOTABLE & QUOTABLE

The first thing you should always do before your puppy comes home is to lie on the ground and look around. You want to be able to see everything your puppy is going to see. For the puppy, the world is one big chew toy.

—Cathleen Stamm, rescue volunteer in San Diego, Calif.

likely to be the first time he has been in a car. The last thing you want to do is smother your Yorkshire Terrier, as this will only frighten him further. This is not to say that human contact is not extremely necessary at this stage because this is the time when a connection between the pup and his human family is formed. Gentle petting and soothing words should help console your Yorkshire Terrier, as well as just putting him down and letting him explore on his own (under your watchful eye, of course).

Your pup may approach the family members or may busy himself with exploring for a while. Gradually, each person should

SMART TIP!

9-1-1! If you don't know whether the plant or food or "stuff" your Yorkie just ate is toxic to dogs, you can call the ASPCA's Animal Poison Control Center (888-426-4435). Be prepared to provide your puppy's age and weight, his symptoms—if any—and how much of the plant, chemical, or substance he ingested, as well as how long ago you think he came into contact with the substance. The ASPCA charges a consultation fee for this service.

Keeping your Yorkie safe in the home means looking at the world from his eye level.

spend some time with the pup, one at a time, crouching down to get as close to the Yorkshire Terrier's level as possible and letting him sniff their hands before petting him gently. He definitely needs human attention, and he needs to be touched; this is how to form an immediate bond. Just remember that the pup is experiencing a lot of things for the first time, at the same time. There are new people, new noises, new smells, and new things to investigate, so be gentle, be affectionate, and be as comforting as you can be.

PUP'S FIRST NIGHT HOME

You have traveled home with your new charge safely in his crate. He may have already been to the vet for a thorough check-up—he's been weighed, his papers examined, perhaps he's even been vaccinated and wormed as well. Your Yorkshire Terrier has met and licked the whole family, including the excited children and the less-than-happy cat. He's explored his area, his new bed, the yard, and anywhere else he's permitted. He's eaten his first meal at home and relieved himself in the proper place. Your Yorkie has heard lots of new sounds, smelled new friends, and seen more of the outside world than ever before.

This was just the first day! He's worn out and is ready for bed—or so you think! Remember, this is your puppy's first night to sleep alone. His mother and littermates are no longer at paw's length, and he's scared, cold, and lonely. Be reassuring to your new family member. This is not the time to spoil your Yorkshire Terrier and give

Did You Know? Everyone who rides in your car has to buckle up—even your Yorkshire Terrier! Your dog can travel in the car inside her crate, or you can use a doggie seat belt. These look like harnesses that attach to your car's seat-belt system.

in to his inevitable whining.

Puppies whine. They whine to let others know where they are and hopefully to get company out of it. Place your pup in his new bed or crate in his room and close the door. Mercifully, he may fall asleep without a peep. If the inevitable occurs, ignore the whining; he is fine. Do not give in and visit the pup. He will fall asleep eventually.

Many breeders recommend placing a piece of bedding from his former home in his new bed so that he recognizes the scent of his littermates. Others still advise placing a

Yorkies need their own beds where they can get comfy.

Playing with toys from puppyhood encourages good behavior and social skills throughout the dog's life. A happy, playful dog is a content and well-adjusted one. Also, because all puppies chew to soothe their gums and help loosen puppy teeth, they should always have easy access to several different toys.—dog trainer and author Harrison Forbes of Savannah, Tenn.

hot water bottle in his bed for warmth. The latter may be a good idea provided the pup doesn't attempt to suckle; he'll get good and wet and may not fall asleep so fast.

Your terrier's first night can be somewhat terrifying for him *and* his new family. Remember that you set the tone of nighttime at your house. Unless you want to play with your pup every night at 10 p.m., midnight, and 2 a.m., don't initiate the habit. Your family will thank you, and so will your pup!

SHOPPING FOR A YORKSHIRE

It's fun shopping for a new puppy. From training to feeding and sleeping to playing, your new Yorkshire Terrier will need a few items to make life comfy, easy, and fun. Be prepared and visit your local pet-supply

Funny Bone

To err is human, to forgive *canine.*
—Anonymous

store before you bring home your new family member.

◆ **Collar and ID tag:** Accustom your dog to wearing a collar the first day you bring him home. Not only will a collar and ID tag help your pup in the event that he becomes lost, but collars are also an important training tool. If your Yorkie gets into trouble, the collar will act as a handle, helping you

Though your dog may be a bit lonely when you first take him from the breeder, he'll soon learn to love his new home!

divert him to a more appropriate behavior. Make sure the collar fits snugly enough so that your Yorkie cannot wriggle out of it, but is loose enough so that it will not be uncomfortably tight around his neck. You should be able to fit a finger between the pup and the collar. Collars come in many styles, but for starting out, a simple buckle collar with an easy-release snap works great.

◆ **Leash:** For training or just for taking a stroll down the street, a leash is your Yorkie's vehicle to explore the outside world. Like collars, leashes come in a variety of styles and materials. A six-foot nylon leash is a

popular choice because it is lightweight and durable. As your pup grows and gets used to walking on the leash, you may want to purchase a flexible leash. These leads allow you to extend the length to give the dog a broader area to explore or to shorten the length to keep the dog closer to you.

◆ **Bowls:** Your Yorkshire Terrier will need

Above all other items, the most important thing your Yorkie needs is your love and attention.

two bowls: one for water and one for food. You may want two sets of bowls, one for inside and one for outside, depending on where the dog will be fed and where she will be spending time. Bowls should be sturdy enough so that they don't tip over easily. (Most have reinforced bottoms that prevent tipping.) Bowls usually are made of metal, ceramic, or plastic, and should be easy to clean.

◆ **Crate:** A crate is multipurpose. It serves as a bed, house-training tool, and travel carrier. It also is the ideal doggie den—a bedroom of sorts—that your Yorkshire Terrier can retire to when he wants to rest or just needs a break. The crate should be large enough for your Yorkshire Terrier to stand in, turn around, and lie down. You don't want any more room than this—especially if

you're planning on using the crate to house-train your dog—because he will eliminate in one corner and lie down in another. Get a crate that is big enough for your dog when he is an adult. Then use dividers to limit the space when he's a puppy.

◆ **Bed:** A plush doggie bed will make sleeping and resting more comfortable for your Yorkie. Dog beds come in all shapes, sizes, and colors, but your dog just needs one that is soft and large enough for him to stretch out on. Because puppies and rescue dogs often don't come house-trained, it's helpful to buy a bed that can be washed easily. If your Yorkie will be sleeping in a crate, a nice crate pad and a small blanket that he can "burrow" in will help him feel more at home. Replace the blanket if it becomes ragged and starts to fall apart because your Yorkie's nails could get caught in it.

◆ **Gate:** Similar to those used for toddlers, gates help keep your Yorkshire Terrier confined to one room or area when you can't supervise him. Gates also work to keep your dog out of areas you don't want him in. Gates are available in many styles. For Yorkies, make sure the one you choose has openings small enough so your tiny puppy can't squeeze through the bars or any openings.

◆ **Toys:** Keep your dog occupied and entertained by providing him with an array of fun toys. Teething puppies like to chew—in fact, chewing is a physical need for pups as they are teething—and everything from your shoes to the leather couch to the Oriental rug are fair game. Divert your Yorkie's chewing instincts with durable toys like bones made of nylon or hard rubber. Other fun toys include rope toys, treat-dispensing toys and balls. Make sure the toys and bones don't have any small parts that could break off and be swallowed, causing your dog to choke. Stuffed toys are popular, but they can become destuffed, and an overly excited puppy may ingest the stuffing or the squeaker. Check your Yorkie's toys regularly and replace them if they become frayed or show signs of wear.

When you bring home your new family member, remember that your home is now also his home.

◆ **Cleaning supplies:** Until your Yorkie pup is house-trained, you will be doing a lot of cleaning. Accidents will occur, which is acceptable in the beginning because the puppy doesn't know any better. All you can do is be prepared to clean up any accidents. Old rags, towels, newspapers, and a stain and odor remover are good to have on hand.

BEYOND THE BASICS

The items previously discussed are the bare necessities. You will find out what else you need as you go along—grooming supplies, flea/tick protection, etc. These things will vary depending on your situation, but it is important that you have everything you need to make your Yorkie comfortable in his new home.

it's a Fact
Traditional baby gates are perfect for securing a laundry room or bathroom, enabling you to keep your Yorkshire Terrier safely within view and out from under your feet—yet still part of the family—while you're fixing dinner or helping the kids with homework.

Some ordinary household items make great toys for your Yorkie—as long you make sure they are safe. You will find a list of homemade toys at **DogChannel.com/Club-Yorkie**

HOUSE-TRAINING

Yorkies are notorious for being difficult to house-train. In fact, lots of small dogs seem to offer this challenge. There are several reasons for this: It's easier to miss a small dog's "I gotta go" signals; smaller dog, smaller mess; messes are easier to miss; etc. It may also be true that because a small dog's organs are smaller, they don't have the capacity to hold it for as long as a big dog.

Muriel Campanella of Woodside, N.Y., who bred Yorkies for thirty years, advises letting the Yorkie decide where he wants to go and letting that be his potty spot. "Let them think it's their idea," she counsels. Yorkie owner Lynn Hoover, from Pittsburgh, Pa., acknowledges that "it takes lifelong vigilance to keep them house-trained. They easily forget that the yard is their human's preferred spot, not the living-room carpet."

The answer to successful house-training is total supervision and management—crates, tethers, exercise pens, and leashes—until you know your dog has developed substrate preferences for outside surfaces (grass, gravel, cement) instead of carpet, tile, or hardwood, and knows that potty happens outside.

it's a Fact

Ongoing house-training difficulties may indicate your puppy has a health problem, warranting a veterinary checkup. A urinary infection, parasites, a virus, and other nasty issues greatly affect your puppy's ability to hold pee or poop.

Because of their small sizes, some Yorkies are trained to potty in a designated area indoors.

IN THE BEGINNING

For the first two to three weeks of a Yorkshire Terrier puppy's life, his mother helps him to eliminate. The mother also keeps the whelping box or "nest area" clean for her family. When the puppies begin to walk around and eat on their own, they choose where they eliminate for themselves. You can train your Yorkshire Terrier puppy to relieve himself wherever you choose, but this must be somewhere suitable. You should bear in mind from the outset that when your puppy is old enough to go out in public places, any canine deposits must be removed at once. You will always have to carry with you a small plastic bag or "poop-scoop."

Outdoor training includes such surfaces as grass, soil, and concrete. Indoor training usually means training your dog on newspaper. When deciding on the surface and location that you will want your Yorkie to use, be sure it is going to be permanent. Training your dog to grass and then changing your mind

Did You Know?

Cleaning accidents properly with an enzyme solution will dramatically reduce the time it takes to house-train your dog because he won't be drawn back to the same areas.

two months later is extremely difficult for dog and owner.

Next, choose the command you will use each and every time you want your puppy to void. "Let's go," "hurry up," and "potty" are examples of commands commonly used by smart dog owners.

Get in the habit of giving the puppy your chosen relief command before you take him out. That way, when he becomes an adult, you will be able to determine if he wants to go out when you ask him. A confirmation will be signs of interest, such as wagging his tail, watching you intently, and going to the door.

LET'S START WITH THE CRATE

Clean animals by nature, dogs keenly dislike soiling where they sleep and eat. This fact makes a crate a useful tool for housetraining. When purchasing a new crate, consider that a correctly sized one will allow adequate room for an adult dog to stand full-height, lie on his side without scrunching, and turn around easily. If debating plastic versus wire crates, short-haired breeds sometimes prefer the warmer, draft-blocking quality of plastic, while furry dogs often like the cooling airflow of a wire crate.

Some crates come equipped with a movable wall that reduces the interior size to

Toy dogs are notorious for being difficult to house-train. Some of the reasons stem from their early experiences. Dogs who are raised in pens where they're forced to potty inside tend to be indiscriminate about where they go later in life. In fact, as adults, dogs tend to prefer using the same type of surface they pottied on as puppies.

provide enough space for your puppy to stand, turn, and lie down, while not allowing room to soil one end and sleep in the other. The problem is that if your puppy goes potty in the crate anyway, the divider forces him to lie in his own excrement.

This can work against you by desensitizing your pup against his normal, instinctive revulsion to resting where he's eliminated. If scheduling permits you or a responsible family member to clean the crate soon after it's soiled, feel free to use this aid, as limiting crate size does encourage your puppy to hold it. Otherwise, give him enough room to move away from an unclean area until he's better able to control his elimination.

Needless to say, not every puppy adheres to this guideline. If your puppy moves along at a faster pace, thank your lucky stars. Should he progress slower, accept it and remind yourself that he'll improve. Be aware that pups frequently hold it longer at night than during the day. Just because your Yorkshire Terrier puppy sleeps for six or more hours through the night, does not mean he can hold it that long during the more active daytime hours.

One last bit of advice on the crate: Place it in the corner of a room with higher traffic, such as the family room or kitchen. Social and curious by nature, dogs like to feel included in family happenings. Creating a quiet retreat by putting the crate in an unused area may seem like a good idea, but results in your puppy feeling insecure and isolated. Watching his people pop in and out of the crate room reassures your puppy that he's not forgotten.

A PUPPY'S NEEDS

Your Yorkie needs to relieve himself after play periods, after each meal, after he has been sleeping, and any time he indi-

Training your dog to love his crate will help when it comes to potty time.

Reward your pup with a high-value treat immediately after he pottys to reinforce going in the proper location, then play for a short time afterward. This teaches that good things happen after pottying outside!—Victoria Schade, certified pet dog trainer, from Annandale, Va.

Puppies will need to eliminate more often than adult dogs.

cates that he is looking for a place to urinate or defecate.

The urinary and intestinal tract muscles of very young puppies are not fully developed. Therefore, like human babies, puppies need to relieve themselves frequently. Take your pup out often—every hour for an eight-week-old—and always immediately after sleeping and eating. The older the puppy, the less often he will need to relieve himself. Finally, as a mature healthy adult, he will require only three to five relief trips per day.

HOUSING HELPS

Because the types of housing and control you provide for your pup have a direct relationship on the success of house-training, smart owners consider the both aspects before beginning training.

Taking a new puppy home and turning him loose in your house can be compared to turning a child loose in a sports arena and telling the child that the place is all his! The sheer enormity of the place would be too much for him to handle.

Instead, offer the puppy clearly defined areas where he can play, sleep, eat, and live. A room of the house where the family gathers is the most obvious choice. Puppies are social animals and need to feel like they are a part of the pack from the start. Hearing your voice, watching you while you are doing things and smelling you nearby are all positive reinforcers that he is a member of your pack. Usually a family room, the kitchen or a nearby adjoining breakfast area is ideal for providing safety and security for puppy and owner.

Within that room, there should be a smaller area that the puppy can call his own. An alcove, a wire or fiberglass dog crate, or a fenced (not boarded!) corner from which he can view the activities of his new family will be fine. The size of the area or crate is the key factor here. The area must be large enough for your Yorkie to lie down and stretch out his little body, yet small enough so that he cannot relieve himself at one end and sleep at the other without coming into contact with his droppings before he is fully trained to relieve himself outside.

Dogs are, by nature, clean animals and will not remain close to their relief areas unless forced to do so. In those cases, they then become dirty dogs and usually remain that way for life.

SMART TIP!

When proximity prevents you from going home at lunch or when you spend longer days at work, make alternative arrangements for getting your puppy out. Hire a pet sitting or walking service, or enlist the aid of an obliging neighbor willing to help.

The designated area should be lined with clean bedding and a toy. Water must always be available, in a nonspill container, once the dog is reliably house-trained.

IN CONTROL

By control, we mean helping the puppy to create a lifestyle pattern that will be compatible to that of his human pack (you!). Just as we guide little children to learn our way of

Teaching your dog where and when to potty takes patience and persistence.

life, we must show the puppy when it is time to play, eat, sleep, exercise, and even entertain himself.

Your puppy should always sleep in his crate. He should also learn that, during times of household confusion and excessive activity, such as at breakfast when family members are preparing for the day, he can play by himself in relative safety and comfort in his designated area. Each time you leave the puppy alone, he should understand exactly where he is to stay.

Puppies are chewers. They cannot tell the difference between lamp cords, television wires, shoes, or table legs. Chewing into a television wire, for example, can be fatal to the puppy, while a shorted wire can start a fire in the house.

If your Yorkie puppy chews on the arm of the chair when he is alone, you will probably discipline him angrily when you get home. Thus, he makes the association that your coming home means he is going to be punished. (He will not remember chewing the chair and is incapable of making the association of the discipline with his naughty deed.)

Other times of excitement, such as family parties, can be fun for your Yorkie, providing that he can view the activities from the security of his designated area. He is not underfoot, and he is not being fed all sorts of tidbits that will probably cause him stomach distress, yet he still feels a part of the fun.

SCHEDULE A SOLUTION

A puppy should be taken to his relief area each time he is released from his designated area, after meals, after play sessions, and when he first awakens in the morning (at age eight weeks, this can mean 5 a.m.!). Your Yorkie will indicate that he's ready "to go" by circling or sniffing busily—do not misinterpret these signs. For a puppy younger than ten weeks of age, a routine of taking him out every hour is necessary. As the puppy grows, he will be able to wait for longer periods of time.

Keep trips to his relief area short. Stay no more than five or six minutes and then return to the house. If he goes during that time, praise him lavishly and take him indoors immediately. If he does not, but he has an accident when you go back indoors, pick

Do not free-feed [leaving food out all the time]. Instead, feed your puppy on a consistent, regular schedule. If you know when it goes in, you can better predict when it'll come out.

—Denise Nord, certified pet dog trainer and owner of Canine Connection Training in Rogers, Minn.

him up immediately, say "No! No!" and return to his relief area. Wait a few minutes, then return to the house again. Never hit a puppy or rub his face in urine or excrement when he has had an accident.

Once indoors, put the puppy in his crate until you have had time to clean up his accident. Then release him to the family area and watch him more closely than before. Chances are, his accident was a result of your not picking up his signal or waiting too long before offering him the opportunity to relieve himself. Never hold a grudge against the puppy for accidents.

Let the puppy learn that going outdoors means it is time to relieve himself, not to play. Once trained, he will be able to play indoors and outdoors and still differentiate between the times for play versus the times for relief.

Help your Yorkshire Terrier develop regular hours for naps, being alone, playing by himself, and just resting, all in his crate. Encourage him to entertain himself while you are busy with your activities. Let him learn that having you nearby is comforting, but it is not your main purpose in life to provide him with undivided attention.

Each time you put your puppy in his own area, use the same command, whatever suits you best. Soon he will run to his crate or special area when he hears you say those words.

Crate-training provides safety for you, the puppy and the home. It also provides the puppy with a feeling of security, and that helps the puppy achieve self-confidence and clean habits.

Remember that one of the primary ingredients in house-training your puppy is control. Regardless of your lifestyle, there will always be occasions when you will need to have a place where your dog can stay and be happy and safe. Crate-training is the answer for now and in the future.

A few key elements are really all you need for successful housebreaking method: consistency, frequency, praise, control, and supervision. By following these procedures with a normal, healthy Yorkie, you and your puppy will soon be past the stage of accidents and ready to move on to a full and rewarding life together.

it's a
Fact

Dogs are descendants of wolves. So you can think of his crate as a modern-day den.

Are you having house-training problems with your Yorkshire Terrier? Ask other Yorkie owners for advice and tips. Log onto **DogChannel.com/Club-Yorkie** and click on "community."

CHAPTER 6

VET VISITS AND

EVERYDAY CARE

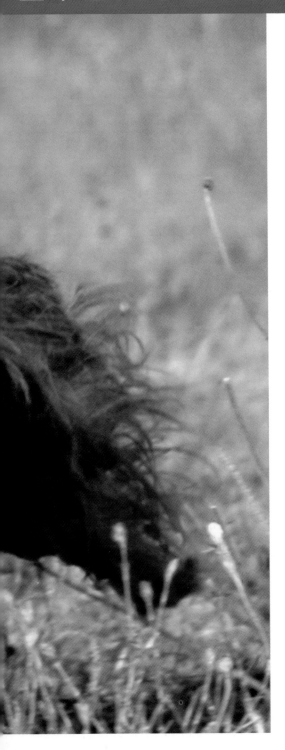

Selecting a veterinarian should be based on his skills with dogs, and, if possible, experience with Yorkshire Terriers. It will be helpful if the vet is based nearby, too, because you might have an emergency or need to make multiple visits for treatments.

FIRST STEP: SELECT THE RIGHT VET

All licensed veterinarians are capable of dealing with routine medical issues such as infections and injuries, as well as the promotion of health (for example, by vaccinations). If the problem affecting your dog is more complex, your veterinarian will refer you to someone with more detailed knowledge of what is wrong. This usually will be a specialist who is a veterinary dermatologist, veterinary ophthalmologist, etc., whatever field you require.

Veterinary procedures are very costly and, as the treatments available improve, they are going to become more expensive. It is quite acceptable to discuss matters of cost with your vet; if there is more than one treatment option, cost may be a factor in deciding which route to take.

Smart owners look for a veterinarian before they actually need one. For newbie pet owners, ideally start looking for a veterinarian a month or two before you bring home your new Yorkie puppy. That will give you time to meet candidate veterinarians, check out the condition of the clinic, and see who you feel comfortable with. If you already have a pet, look sooner rather than later, preferably not in the midst of a veterinary health crisis.

Second, define the criteria that are important to you. Points to consider or investigate:

Convenience: Proximity to your home, extended hours, or drop-off services are helpful for people who work regular business hours, have a busy schedule, or don't want to drive far. If you have mobility issues, finding a vet who makes house calls or a service that provides pet transport might be particularly important.

Size: The one-person practice ensures that you will always be dealing with the same vet during each and every visit. "That person can really get to know you and your dog," says Bernadine Cruz, D.V.M., of Laguna Hills Animal Hospital in Laguna Hills, Calif. The downside, though, is the sole practitioner does not have the immediate input of another veterinarian, and if your vet becomes ill or takes time off, you are out of luck.

The multiple-doctor practice offers consistency if your Yorkie needs to come in unexpectedly on a day when your veterinarian isn't there. Additionally, a vet can quickly consult with his colleagues within the clinic if he's unsure about a diagnosis or a treatment.

If you find a veterinarian within that practice who you really like, you can make your appointments with that individual, establishing the same kind of bond that you would with the solo practitioner.

Appointment Policies: Some practices are strictly by-appointment only, which could minimize your wait time. However, if a sudden problem arises with your Yorkie and the veterinarians are booked up, they might not be able to squeeze your pet in that day. Some clinics are drop-in only—great for impromptu or crisis visits, but without scheduling may involve longer waits to see the next available veterinarian—whoever is open, not someone in particular. Some practices maintain an appointment schedule but also keep slots open throughout the day for walk-ins, offering the best of both worlds.

Basic vs. State-of-the-Art vs. Full Service: A practice with high-tech equipment offers greater diagnostic capabilities and treatment options, important for tricky or dif-

Picking the right vet is one of the most important decisions you'll make for the lifelong health of your new family member. Make sure you ask the right questions to ensure that your vet is knowledgeable not only about dogs, but Yorkshire Terriers in particular. Download a list of questions to ask potential vets by logging on to **DogChannel.com/Club-Yorkie**—just click on "downloads."

ficult cases. However, the cost of pricey equipment is passed along to the client, so you could pay more for routine procedures—the bulk of most pets' appointments. Some practices offer boarding, grooming, training classes, and other services on the premises—conveniences some pet owners appreciate.

Fees and Payment Polices: How much is a routine office call? If there is a significant price difference, ask why. If you intend to carry health insurance on your Yorkie or want to pay by credit card, make sure the candidate clinic accepts those payment options.

FIRST VET VISIT

It is much easier, less costly, and more effective to practice preventive medicine than to fight bouts of illness and disease. Properly bred puppies of all breeds come from parents who were selected based upon their genetic disease profile. The puppies' mother should have been vaccinated, free of all internal and external parasites, and properly nourished. For these reasons, a visit to the veterinarian who cared for the dam (mother) is recommended if at all possible. The dam passes disease resistance to her puppies, which should last from eight to ten weeks. Unfortunately, she can also pass on parasites and infection. This is why knowledge about her health is useful in learning more about the health of the puppies.

Now that you have your Yorkshire Terrier puppy home safe and sound, it's time to arrange your pup's first trip to the veterinarian. Perhaps the breeder can recommend someone in the area who specializes in Yorkshire Terriers, or maybe you know other Yorkie owners who can suggest a good vet. Either way, you should make an appointment within a couple of days of

When a veterinarian injects a vaccine into your dog, the process is called "vaccination." How your dog's immune system responds to the vaccine is called "immunization."

Make sure your Yorkie feels as good as he looks!

bringing home your puppy. If possible, see if you can stop for this first vet appointment before going home.

The pup's first vet visit will consist of an overall examination to make sure that the pup does not have any problems that are not apparent to you. The veterinarian also will set up a schedule for the pup's vaccinations; the breeder will inform you of which ones the dog has already received, and the vet can continue from there.

The puppy also will have his teeth examined and have his skeletal conformation and general health checked prior to certification by the veterinarian. Puppies in certain breeds have problems with their kneecaps, cataracts and other eye problems, heart murmurs, and undescended testicles. They may also have personality

problems, and your veterinarian might have training in temperament evaluation.

VACCINATION SCHEDULING

Most vaccinations are given by injection and should only be given by a veterinarian. Both you and the vet should keep a record of the date of the injection, the identification of the vaccine, and the amount given. Some vets give a first vaccination at eight weeks of age, but most dog breeders prefer the course

Yorkies need to be taken care of just like any member of your family.

NOTABLE & QUOTABLE

These little breeds sometimes retain their baby teeth, and when that happens, the veterinarian has to put the dog under anesthesia to remove those teeth. Instead of putting them under twice—once for the early spay or neuter and then again to remove retained baby teeth—I recommend doing the spay or neuter after age six months when all the adult teeth are in. Then, while the puppy is anesthetized, the veterinarian can look for extra teeth and remove them at the same time.

—Bernadine Cruz, D.V.M., of Laguna Hills Animal Hospital in California

A good wellness plan for your Yorkie will include several trips to the vet for vaccines.

not to commence until about ten weeks because of interaction with the antibodies produced by the mother. The vaccination scheduling is usually based on a fifteen-day cycle. You must take your vet's advice as to when to vaccinate, as this may differ according to the vaccine used.

The usual vaccines contain immunizing doses of several different viruses such as distemper, parvovirus, parainfluenza, and hepatitis. There are other vaccines available when the puppy is at risk. You should rely on your vet's advice. This is especially true for the booster immunizations. Most vaccination programs require a booster when the puppy is a year old and once a year thereafter. In some cases, circumstances may require more frequent immunizations.

Kennel cough, more formally known as tracheobronchitis, is immunized against with a vaccine that is sprayed into the dog's nostrils. Kennel cough is usually included in routine vaccination, but it is often not as effective as the vaccines for other major diseases.

Your veterinarian probably will recommend that your Yorkshire Terrier puppy be fully vaccinated before you take him on outings. There are airborne diseases, parasite eggs in the grass, and unexpected visits from other dogs that might be dangerous to your puppy's health. Other dogs are the most harmful reservoir of pathogenic organisms, as everything they have can be transmitted to your puppy.

Five Months to One Year of Age: Unless you intend to breed or show your dog, neutering the puppy at six months of age is recommended. Discuss this with your veterinarian. Neutering/spaying has proven to be beneficial to male and female puppies, respectively. Besides eliminating the possibility of pregnancy, it inhibits (but does not prevent) breast cancer in females and prostate cancer in male dogs.

Your veterinarian should provide your Yorkie puppy with a thorough dental evaluation at six months of age, ascertaining whether all his permanent teeth have erupted properly. A home dental care regimen should be initiated at six months, including brushing weekly and providing good dental devices (such as nylon bones). Regular dental care promotes healthy teeth, fresh breath, and a longer life.

Dogs Older Than One Year: Continue to visit the veterinarian at least once a year. There is no such disease as "old age," but bodily functions do change with age. The eyes and ears are no longer as efficient. Liver, kidney, and intestinal functions often decline. Proper dietary changes, recommended by

Yorkshire Terriers can develop luxated patellas—popped kneecaps. Affected Yorkies will be more prone to degenerative joint disease, or they may rupture the ligaments in their knees, especially if they become overweight.

—*Bernadine Cruz, D.V.M., of Laguna Hills Animal Hospital in California*

your veterinarian, can make life more pleasant for your aging Yorkshire Terrier and you.

EVERYDAY HAPPENINGS

Keeping your Yorkshire Terrier healthy is a matter of keen observation and quick action when necessary. Knowing what's normal for your dog will help you recognize signs of trouble before they blossom into a full-blown emergency situation.

Even if the problem is minor, such as a cut or scrape, you'll want to care for it immediately to prevent subsequent infections, as well as to ensure that your dog doesn't make it worse by chewing or scratching at it.

Here's what to do for common, minor injuries or illnesses, and how to recognize and deal with emergencies.

Cuts and Scrapes: For a cut or scrape that's half an inch or smaller, clean the wound with saline solution or warm water and use tweezers to remove any splinters or other debris. Apply antibiotic ointment. No bandage is necessary unless the wound is on a paw, which can pick up dirt when your dog walks on it. Deep cuts with lots of bleeding or those caused by glass or some other object should be treated by your veterinarian.

Cold Symptoms: Dogs don't actually get colds, but they can get illnesses that have similar symptoms, such as coughing, a runny nose, or sneezing. Dogs cough for

Just like with infants, puppies need a series of vaccinations to ensure that they stay healthy during their first year of life. Download a vaccination chart from **DogChannel.com/Club-Yorkie** that you can fill out for your terrier.

The vet will be an important part of your
Yorkie's life, so it's vital to establish
a good relationship from the beginning.

any number of reasons, from respiratory infections to inhaled irritants to congestive heart failure. Take your Yorkie to the veterinarian for prolonged coughing, or coughing accompanied by labored breathing, runny eyes or nose, or bloody phlegm.

A runny nose that continues for more than several hours requires veterinary attention, as well. If your Yorkie sneezes, he may have some mild nasal irritation that will resolve on its own, but frequent sneezing, especially if it's accompanied by a runny nose, may indicate anything from allergies to an infection to something stuck in the nose.

Vomiting and Diarrhea: Sometimes dogs suffer minor gastric upsets when they eat a new type of food, eat too much, eat the contents of the trash can, or become excited or anxious. Give your Yorkshire Terrier's stomach a rest by withholding food for twelve hours, and then feeding him a bland diet such as baby food or rice and chicken, gradually returning your Yorkie to his normal food. Projectile vomiting, or vomiting or diarrhea that continues for more than forty-eight hours, is another matter. If this happens, take your Yorkie to the veterinarian.

Take your Yorkie to the vet each year for a check-up, not just when he isn't feeling good.

No matter how careful you are with your darling Yorkie, sometimes unexpected injuries happen. Be prepared for any emergency by creating a canine first-aid kit. Find out what essentials you need on **DogChannel.com/Club-Yorkie**—click on "downloads."

In all, the Yorkshire Terrier is a healthy, adaptable dog. Smart owners are well advised to investigate each of the disorders mentioned in this chapter and discuss them with the vet. The better informed an owner is, the healthier and long-lived his Yorkshire Terrier will be.

SKIN PROBLEMS

Veterinarians are consulted by dog owners for skin problems more than any other group of diseases or maladies. A dog's skin is as sensitive, if not more so, as human skin, and both suffer almost the same ailments (though the occurrence of acne in most breeds of dog is rare!). For this reason, veterinary dermatology has developed into a specialty practiced by many veterinarians.

Because many skin problems have visual symptoms that are almost identical, it requires the skill of an experienced veterinary dermatologist to identify and cure many of the more severe skin disorders. Pet-supply stores sell many treatments for skin problems, but most of them are directed at symptoms and not at the underlying problem(s). If your Yorkie is suffering from a skin disorder, seek professional assistance as quickly as possible. As with

it's a Fact

Dogs can get Lyme disease, Rocky Mountain spotted fever, tick bite paralysis, and many other diseases from ticks.

SMART TIP! **Keep your Yorkies coat and skin clean.** Regular grooming removes dead hair, dead skin, dirt and mats, which can trap oil and moisture against the skin, predisposing the skin to infection.

all diseases, the earlier a problem is identified and treated, the more likely that the cure will be successful. There are active programs being undertaken by many veterinary pharmaceutical manufacturers to solve most, if not all, of the common skin problems in dogs.

PARASITE BITES

Insect bites itch, erupt, and may even become infected. Dogs have the same reaction to fleas, ticks, and/or mites. When an insect lands on you, you can whisk it away with your hand. Unfortunately, when a dog is bitten by a flea, tick, or mite, he can only scratch it away or bite it. By the time your Yorkshire Terrier has been bitten, the parasite has done its damage. It may also have laid eggs, which will cause further problems. The itching from parasite bites is probably due to the saliva injected into the site when the parasite sucks the dog's blood.

AIRBORNE ALLERGIES

Just as humans suffer from hay fever during the pollinating season, many dogs suffer from the same allergies. When the pollen count is high, your Yorkie might suffer, but don't expect him to sneeze or have a runny nose like a human. Dogs react to pollen allergies in the same way they react to fleas; they scratch and bite themselves. Dogs, like humans, can be tested for allergens. Discuss the testing with your vet.

AUTO-IMMUNE ILLNESS

An auto-immune illness is one in which the immune system overacts and does not recognize parts of the affected person. Instead, the immune system starts to react as if these parts were foreign and need to be destroyed. An example is rheumatoid arthritis, which occurs when the body does not recognize the joints, and this leads to a very painful and damaging reaction in the joints. This has nothing to do with age, so it can occur in puppies. The wear-and-tear arthritis in older people or dogs is called osteoarthritis.

Lupus is another auto-immune disease that affects dogs as well as people. It can take variable forms, affecting the kidneys, bones, and the skin. It can be fatal, so it is treated with steroids, which can themselves have very significant side effects. Steroids

calm down the allergic reaction to the body's tissues, which helps the lupus, but also calms down the body's reaction to real foreign substances such as bacteria, and also thins the skin and bones.

FOOD ALLERGIES

Feeding your Yorkie properly is very important. An incorrect diet could affect your dog's health, behavior, and nervous system, possibly making a normal dog an aggressive one. The result of a good—or bad—diet is most visible in a dog's skin and coat, but internal organs are affected, too.

Dogs are allergic to many foods that are popular and highly recommended by breeders and veterinarians. Changing the brand of food may not eliminate the problem if the ingredient to which your dog is allergic is contained in the new brand.

Recognizing a food allergy can be difficult. Humans often have rashes or swelling of the lips or eyes when they eat foods they are allergic to. Dogs do not usually develop rashes, but they react the same way they do to an airborne or bite allergy—they itch, scratch, and bite. While pollen allergies and parasite bites are usually seasonal, food allergies are year-round problems.

Diagnosis of a food allergy is based on a two- to four-week dietary trial with a home-cooked diet fed to the exclusion of all other foods. The diet should consist of boiled rice or potato with a source of protein that your Yorkie has never eaten before, such as fresh or frozen fish, lamb, or even something as exotic as pheasant. Water has to be the only drink, and it is important that no other foods are fed during this trial. If your dog's condition improves, try the original diet again to see if

Just like humans, dogs can suffer from allergies, too.

the itching resumes. If it does, then your dog is allergic to his original diet. You must find a diet that does not distress your dog's skin. Start with a commercially available hypoallergenic diet or the homemade diet that you created for the allergy trial.

Food intolerance is the inability of the dog to completely digest certain foods. This occurs because the dog does not have the chemicals (enzymes) necessary to digest some foodstuffs. All puppies have the enzymes necessary to digest canine milk, but some dogs do not have the enzymes to digest cow milk, resulting in loose bowels, stomach pains, and the passage of gas.

Dogs often do not have the enzymes to digest soy or other beans. The treatment is to exclude these foods from your Yorkshire Terrier's diet.

EXTERNAL PARASITES

Fleas: Of all the problems to which dogs are prone, none is better known and more frustrating than fleas. Flea infestation is relatively simple to cure but difficult to prevent.

To control flea infestation, you have to understand the flea's life cycle. Fleas are often thought of as a summertime problem, but centrally heated homes have made fleas a year-round problem. The most effective method of flea control is a two-stage approach: kill the adult fleas, then control the development of pre-adult fleas. Unfortunately, no single active ingredient is effective against all stages of the flea life cycle.

Treating fleas should be a two-pronged attack. First, the environment needs to be treated; this includes carpets and furniture,

External parasites can make your dog miserable, so be sure to prevent them before they crop up.

especially your Yorkie's bedding and areas underneath furniture. The environment should be treated with a household spray containing an insect growth regulator and an insecticide to kill the adult fleas. Most IGRs are effective against eggs and larvae; they actually mimic the fleas' own hormones and stop the eggs and larvae from developing into adult fleas. There are currently no treatments available to attack the pupae stage of the life cycle, so the adult insecticide is used to kill the newly hatched adult fleas before they find a host. Most IGRs are active for many months, while adult insecticides are only active for a few days.

When treating with a household spray, vacuum before applying the product. This stimulates as many pupae as possible to hatch into adult fleas. The vacuum cleaner should also be treated with an insecticide to prevent the eggs and larvae that have been collected in the vacuum bag from hatching.

The second stage of treatment is to apply an adult insecticide to your Yorkshire Terrier. Traditionally, this would be in the form of a collar or a spray, but more recent innovations include digestible insecticides that poison the fleas when they ingest the dog's blood. Alternatively, there are drops that, when placed on the back of the dog's neck, spread throughout the hair and skin to kill adult fleas.

Ticks: Though not as common as fleas, ticks are found all over the tropical and temperate world. They don't bite like fleas; they harpoon. They dig their sharp proboscis (nose) into your Yorkie's skin and drink the blood, which is their only food and drink. Ticks are controlled the same way fleas are controlled.

The American dog tick, *Dermacentor variabilis*, may well be the most common dog

tick in many geographical areas, especially those areas where the climate is hot and humid. Most dog ticks have life expectancies of a week to six months, depending on climatic conditions. They can neither jump nor fly, but they can crawl slowly and can range up to sixteen feet to reach a sleeping or unsuspecting dog.

Mites: Just as fleas and ticks can be problematic for your dog, mites can also lead to an itch fit. Microscopic in size, mites are related to ticks and generally take up permanent residence on their host animal—in this case, your Yorkie! The term "mange" refers to any infestation caused by one of the mighty mites, of which there are six varieties that smart dog owners should know.

● *Demodex mites* cause a condition known as demodicosis (sometimes called "red mange" or "follicular mange"), in which the mites live in the dog's hair follicles and sebaceous glands in larger-than-normal numbers. Most dogs recover from this type of mange without any treatment, though topical therapies are commonly prescribed by the vet.

● The *Cheyletiellosis mite* is the hook-mouthed culprit associated with "walking dandruff," a condition that affects dogs as well as cats and rabbits. If untreated, this mange can affect a whole kennel of dogs and can be spread to humans, as well.

● The *Sarcoptes mite* causes intense itching on the dog in the form of a condition known as scabies or sarcoptic mange. Scabies is highly contagious and can be

passed to humans. Sometimes an allergic reaction to the mite worsens the severe itching associated with sarcoptic mange.

● Ear mites, *Otodectes cynotis*, lead to otodectic mange, which commonly affects the outer ear canal of the dog, though other areas can be affected as well. Your vet can prescribe a treatment to flush out the ears and kill any eggs in the ears. A complete month of treatment is necessary to cure this mange.

● Two other mites, less common in dogs, include *Dermanyssus gallinae* (the "poultry" or "red mite") and *Eutrombicula alfreddugesi* (the North American mite associated with trombiculidiasis or chigger infestation). The types of mange caused by both of these mites must be treated by vets.

INTERNAL PARASITES

Most animals—fishes, birds, and mammals, including dogs and humans—have worms and other parasites that live inside their bodies. According to Dr. Herbert R. Axelrod, a fish pathologist, there are two kinds of parasites: dumb and smart. The smart parasites live in peaceful cooperation with their hosts (symbiosis), while the dumb parasites kill their hosts. Most worm infections are relatively easy to control. If they are not controlled, they weaken the host dog to the point that other medical problems occur, but they do not kill the host as dumb parasites would.

Roundworms: Roundworms that infect dogs live in the dog's intestines and shed eggs continually. It has been estimated that a dog produces about six or more ounces of feces every day. Each ounce averages hundreds of thousands of roundworm eggs. There are no known areas in which dogs roam that do not contain roundworm eggs. Because roundworms infect people, too, it is wise to have your dog regularly tested.

Roundworm infection can kill puppies and cause severe problems in adult dogs, as the hatched larvae travel to the lungs and trachea through the bloodstream. Cleanliness is the best preventive for roundworms. Always pick up after your dog and dispose of feces in appropriate receptacles.

Hookworms: Hookworms are dangerous to humans as well as to dogs and cats, and can be the cause of severe anemia due to iron deficiency. The worm uses its teeth to attach itself to the dog's intestines and changes the site of its attachment about six times per day. Each time the worm repositions itself, the dog loses blood and can become anemic.

Symptoms of hookworm infection include dark stools, weight loss, general weakness, pale coloration, and anemia, as well as possible skin problems. Fortunately, hookworms are easily purged with a number of medications that have proven effective. Discuss these with your veterinarian. Most heartworm preventives include a hookworm insecticide, as well.

Humans, can be infected by hookworms through exposure to contaminated feces. Because the worms cannot complete their life cycle on a human, the worms simply infest the skin and cause irritation. As a preventive, use disposable gloves or a "poop-scoop" to pick up your dog's droppings and prevent your dog (or neighborhood cats) from defecating in children's play areas.

Tapeworms: There are many species of tapeworm, all of which are carried by fleas! Fleas are so small that your Yorkshire Terrier could pass them onto your hands, your plate, or your food, making it possible for you to ingest a flea that is carrying tapeworm eggs. While tapeworm infection is not life-threatening in dogs (smart parasite!), it can be the cause of a very serious liver disease in humans.

Whipworms: In North America, whipworms are counted among the most common parasitic worms in dogs. Affected dogs may only experience upset tummies, colic, and diarrhea. These worms, however, can live for months or years in the dog, beginning their larval stage in the small intestine, spending their adult stage in the large intestine and finally passing infective eggs through the dog's feces. The only way to detect whipworms is through a fecal examination, though this is not always foolproof. Treatment for whipworms is tricky, due to the worms' unusual life cycle, and often dogs

A healthy Yorkie has clear eyes, a shiny coat, and an energetic personality.

are reinfected due to exposure to infective eggs on the ground. Cleaning up droppings in your backyard as well as in public places is absolutely essential for sanitation purposes and the health of your dog and others.

Threadworms: Though less common than roundworms, hookworms, and those previously mentioned parasites, threadworms concern dog owners in southwestern United States and the Gulf Coast area where the climate is hot and humid. Living in the small intestine of the dog, this worm measures a mere 2 millimeters and is round in shape. Like the whipworm, the threadworm's life cycle is very complex, and the eggs and larvae are passed through the feces. A deadly disease in humans, threadworms readily infect people, most commonly through the handling of feces. Threadworms are most often seen in young puppies. The most common symptoms include bloody diarrhea and pneumonia. Sick puppies must be isolated and treated immediately; vets recommend a follow-up treatment one month later.

Heartworms: Heartworms are thin, extended worms up to 12 inches long, that live in a dog's heart and the major blood vessels surrounding it. Dogs may have up to 200 heartworms. Symptoms may be loss of energy, loss of appetite, coughing, the development of a pot belly, and anemia.

Heartworms are transmitted by mosquitoes, which drink the blood of infected dogs and take in larvae with the blood. The larvae, called *microfilariae*, develop within the body of the mosquito and are passed on to the next dog bitten after the larvae mature. It takes two to three weeks for the larvae to develop to the infective stage within the body of the mosquito. Dogs are usually treated at about six weeks of age and maintained on a prophylactic dose given monthly.

Blood testing for heartworms is not necessarily indicative of how seriously your dog is infected. Although this is a dangerous disease, it is not easy for a dog to be infected. Discuss the various preventives with your vet, because there are many different types now available. Together you can decide on a safe course of prevention for your dog.

YORKIE EYE DILEMMAS

Your Yorkie's eyes are not only a good indication of his affection and devotion for you, his owner, but also an excellent way of evaluating the dog's health. As in all dogs, the eyes should be clear and bright, a general sign of good health and intelligence. Look for any cloudiness or opacity in the eyes of your dog; this could indicate a problem to bring to your veterinarian's attention. Yorkshire Terriers are prone to some hereditary eye conditions. Among these conditions, the most common are cataracts, progressive retinal atrophy, keratoconjunctivitis sicca, and ulcerative keratitis.

Yorkies tend to develop cataracts after three years of age, most frequently between three and six years. Fortunately, veterinary

it's a **Fact**

In young puppies, roundworms cause bloated bellies, diarrhea, coughing, and vomiting, and are transmitted from the mother (through blood or milk). Affected puppies will not appear as animated as normal puppies. The worms appear spaghetti-like, measuring as long as 6 inches!

advances make it possible for successful cataract surgery to take place. As in humans, the cataracts can be removed by a trained veterinary ophthalmologist.

Progressive retinal atrophy, aka PRA, causes blindness in affected dogs. The Yorkshire Terrier is commonly struck by PRA in the later years, usually around eight years of age, though it can be as early as five and as late as twelve. As the name describes, the deterioration of the retina worsens over time. Affected dogs experience limitations in their sight, but because Yorkies are very adaptive, the owner may not notice that the dog's sight is failing. Usually, PRA has become rather severe by the time the owner is aware that the dog is affected.

Keratoconjunctivitis sicca is abbreviated KCS and is more commonly called "dry eye."

The "dry eye" condition results from the lacrimal glands' failure to produce tears in the eye. The cornea suffers from lack of "wetness," and these dry areas cause damage to the eye. Mucus accumulation around the eyes is the first sign that there is a problem. Treatment is available, which includes antibiotics and other drugs. In unusual cases, surgery can correct the condition. Like PRA, KCS is hereditary and affected Yorkies should not be bred.

The fourth eye condition that affects Yorkies, ulcerative keratitis, also targets the cornea. Infection and ulceration (formation of ulcers) on the cornea are caused by the dog's hair's irritating his eyes. Owners may notice their Yorkies blinking excessively and pawing at their eyes from discomfort, and a watery appearance to the eye. This is not a

Your dog should be cared for as if he were one of the family—because he is!

hereditary condition but merely a result of the Yorkshire Terrier's prominent eyes. The condition can be treated with antibiotics and special applications.

MORE YORKIE HEALTH CONCERNS

Two orthopedic conditions that commonly affect toy dogs and other small breeds are Legg-Calve-Perthes disease and

Did You Know?

By and large, Yorkshire Terriers are bundles of health and energy, a long-lived breed with a normal lifespan of thirteen to fifteen years, with some dogs even reaching the ripe old age of eighteen years.

patellar luxation. Commonly seen in young Yorkies, Legg-Calve-Perthes has a high incidence in the breed. The disease causes lameness in the hip joint, resulting from the collapsing of the femoral head of the leg. Very frequently, in eight or nine out of ten cases, only one leg is affected. It is likely hereditary, though veterinary research is not conclusive.

Patellar luxation, in layperson's terms, means a "slipped kneecap." Although it is hereditary, it is not usually a serious problem. Cases vary greatly depending on the laxity of the patella. In young Yorkies, surgery is commonly recommended before the condition causes arthritis.

When selecting a veterinarian, be sure he has experience with toy breeds, especially Yorkies. A good bedside manner doesn't hurt either!

DINNER

You have probably heard it a thousand times—you are what you eat. Believe it or not, it is very true. For dogs, they are what you feed them because they have little choice in the matter. Even those people who truly want to feed their Yorkshire Terriers the best often can't because they do not know which foods are best for their dogs.

BASIC TYPES

Dog foods are produced in various types: dry, wet (canned), semimoist, fresh packaged, and frozen.

Dry foods are useful for the cost-conscious they tend to be less expensive than the others. They also contain the least fat and the most preservatives. Dry food is bulky and takes longer to eat than other foods, so it's more filling.

Wet food—available in cans or foil pouches—is usually sixty to seventy percent water and is more expensive than dry food, but this isn't a major concern with small dogs such as Yorkies. A palatable source of concentrated nutrition, wet food makes a good supplement for underweight dogs or

it's a **Fact**

Bones can cause gastro-intestinal obstruction and perforation, and may be contaminated with salmonella or E. coli. Leave them in the trash and give your dog a nylon bone toy instead.

those recovering from illness. Some owners add a little wet food to dry food to increase its appeal.

Semimoist food is flavorful but usually contains lots of sugar, which can lead to dental problems and obesity. It's not a good choice for your diminutive dog's main diet.

Likewise, **frozen** food, which is available in cooked and raw forms, is usually more expensive than wet foods. The advantages of frozen food are similar to those of wet foods.

Some manufacturers have developed special foods for small dogs. Some of these contain slightly more protein, fat, and calories than standard foods. Manufacturers contend that small dogs need these additional nutrients to fuel their active lifestyle and revved-up metabolism. In reality, your toy dog may or may not need them; the nutritional needs of dogs vary considerably,

even within the same breed. It's OK to feed your Yorkie small-breed food, but standard food will provide balanced nutrition, too, as long as you feed appropriate amounts tailored to your buddy's needs.

Some dry foods for small dogs have compositions that are identical to those for larger dogs, but the kibble size is smaller to make it easier to chew. Small dogs don't really need smaller kibble, though your dog may prefer it. Many small dogs eat standard-size kibble with no trouble at all.

The amount of food your Yorkie needs depends on a number of factors, such as age, activity level, food quality, reproductive status, and size. What's the easiest way to figure it out? Start with the manufacturer's recommended amount, then adjust it according to your dog's response. For

Active Yorkies needs tons of nutrients, so stock up on healthy treats!

Believe it or not, during your Yorkshire's lifetime, you'll buy a few thousand pounds of dog food! Go to **DogChannel.com/Club-Yorkie** and download a chart that outlines the cost of dog food.

example, feed the recommended amount for a few weeks and your Yorkie loses weight, increase the amount by ten to twenty percent. If your dog gains weight, decrease the amount. It won't take long to determine the amount of food that keeps your little friend in optimal condition.

NUTRITION 101

All Yorkshire Terriers (and all dogs, for that matter) need proteins, carbohydrates, fats, vitamins, and minerals for optimal growth and health.

■ **Proteins** are used for growth and repair of muscles, bones, and other bodily tissues. They're also used for production of antibodies, enzymes, and hormones. All dogs need protein, but it's especially important for puppies because they grow and develop so rapidly. Protein sources include various types of meat, meat meal, meat byproducts, eggs, dairy products, and soybeans.

■ **Carbohydrates** are metabolized into glucose, the body's principal energy source. Carbohydrates are available as sugars, starches, and fiber.

Frozen, dry or wet?
Find the right food
for your Yorkie
(and your wallet).

Dogs of all ages love treats and table food, but these goodies can unbalance your terrier's diet and lead to a weight problem if you don't choose and feed them wisely. Table food, whether fed as a treat or as part of a meal, shouldn't account for more than ten percent of your Yorkie's daily caloric intake. If you plan to give your Yorkie treats, be sure to include "treat calories" when calculating the daily food requirement—so you don't end up with a pudgy pup!

When shopping for packaged treats, look for ones that provide complete nutrition—they're basically dog food in a fun form. Choose crunchy goodies for chewing fun and dental health. Other ideas for tasty treats include:

✓ small chunks of cooked, lean meat
✓ dry dog food morsels
✓ cheese
✓ veggies (cooked, raw or frozen)
✓ breads, crackers, or dry cereal
✓ unsalted, unbuttered, plain, popped popcorn

Some foods, however, can be dangerous and even deadly to a dog. The following items can cause digestive upset (vomiting or diarrhea) or toxic reactions that could be fatal:

✗ **avocados:** can cause gastrointestinal irritation, with vomiting and diarrhea, if eaten in sufficient quantity

✗ **baby food:** may contain onion powder; does not provide balanced nutrition

✗ **chocolate:** contains methylxanthines and theobromine, caffeine-like compounds that can cause vomiting, diarrhea, heart abnormalities, tremors, seizures, and death. Darker chocolates contain higher levels of the toxic compounds.

✗ **eggs, raw:** whites contain an enzyme that prevents uptake of biotin, a B vitamin; may contain salmonella

✗ **garlic (and related foods):** can cause gastrointestinal irritation and anemia if eaten in sufficient quantity

✗ **grapes:** can cause kidney failure if eaten in sufficient quantity (the toxic dose varies from dog to dog)

✗ **macadamia nuts:** can cause vomiting, weakness, lack of coordination, and other problems.

✗ **meat, raw:** may contain harmful bacteria such as salmonella or E. coli

✗ **milk:** can cause diarrhea in some puppies.

✗ **onions (and related foods):** can cause gastrointestinal irritation and anemia if eaten in sufficient quantity

✗ **raisins:** can cause kidney failure if eaten in sufficient quantity (the toxic dose varies from dog to dog)

✗ **yeast bread dough:** can rise in the gastrointestinal tract, causing obstruction; produces alcohol as it rises

• Sugars (simple carbohydrates) are not suitable nutrient sources for dogs.

• Starches—a preferred type of carbohydrates in dog food—are found in a variety of plant products. Starches must be cooked in order to be digested.

• Fiber (cellulose)—also a preferred type of carbohydrate in dog food—isn't digestible but helps the digestive tract function properly.

■ **Fats** are also used for energy and play an important role in skin and coat health, hormone production, nervous system function, and vitamin transport. Fat increases the palatability and the calorie count of puppy/dog food, which can lead to serious health problems, such as obesity, for puppies or dogs that are allowed to overindulge. Some foods contain added amounts of omega fatty

Feeding your dog is part of your daily routine. Take a break and have some fun online and play "Feed the Yorkie," an exclusive game found only on **DogChannel.com/Club-Yorkie**—just click on "fun and games."

JOIN OUR ONLINE
Club Yorkie®

acids such as docosohexaenoic acid, a compound that may enhance brain development and learning in puppies but is not considered an essential nutrient by the Association of American Feed Control Officials (www.aafco.org). Fats used in dog foods include tallow, lard, poultry fat, fish oil and vegetable oils.

■ **Vitamins and minerals** help muscle and nerve functions, bone growth, healing, metabolism, and fluid balance. Especially important for your puppy are calcium, phosphorus, and vitamin D, which must be supplied in the right balance to ensure proper development of bones and teeth.

Just as your Yorkshire Terrier needs proper nutrition from his food, **water** is an essential "nutrient" as well. Water keeps the dog's body properly hydrated and promotes normal function of the body's systems.

During house-training, it is necessary to keep an eye on how much water your Yorkie is drinking, but once he is reliably trained, he should have access to clean, fresh water at all times, especially if you feed dry food. Make sure that your Yorkie's water bowl is clean, and change the water often.

Did You Know?

Because semimoist food contains lots of sugar, it isn't a good selection for your Yorkie's main menu. However, it is great for an occasional yummy snack. Try forming into little meatballs for a once-a-week treat! He'll love ya for it!

Keep sugary foods away from your Yorkie; you don't want to satisfy that sweet tooth.

How can you tell if your Yorkie is fit or fat? When you run your hands down your pal's sides from front to back, you should be able to easily feel his ribs. It's OK if you feel a little body fat (and, of course, a lot of hair), but you should not feel huge fat pads. You should also be able to feel your Yorkie's waist—an indentation behind the ribs.

CHECK OUT THE LABEL

To help you get a feel for what you are feeding your dog, start by taking a look at the label on the package or can. Look for the words "complete and balanced." This tells you that the food meets specific nutritional requirements set by the AAFCO for either adults ("maintenance") or puppies and pregnant/lactating females ("growth and reproduction"). The label must state the group for which it is intended. Because you're feeding a puppy, choose a "growth and reproduction" food.

The label also includes a nutritional analysis, which lists minimum protein, minimum fat, maximum fiber, and maximum moisture content, as well as other information. (You won't find carbohydrate content because it's everything that isn't protein, fat, fiber, and moisture.)

The nutritional analysis refers to crude protein and crude fat—amounts that have been determined in the laboratory. This analysis is technically accurate, but it doesn't tell you anything about digestibility: how much of the particular nutrient your Yorkie can actually use. For information about digestibility, contact the manufacturer (check the label for a telephone number and website address).

Virtually all commercial puppy foods exceed AAFCO's minimal requirements for protein and fat, the two nutrients most commonly evaluated when comparing foods. Protein levels in dry puppy foods usually range from about twenty-six to thirty percent; for canned foods, the values are about nine to thirteen percent. The fat content of dry puppy foods is about twenty percent or more; for canned foods, it's eight percent or more. (Dry food values are larger than canned food values because dry food contains less water; the values are actually similar when compared on a dry matter basis.)

Finally, check the ingredients on the label, which lists the ingredients in descending order by weight. Manufacturers are allowed to list separately different forms of a single ingredient (e.g., ground corn and corn gluten meal). The food may contain things like meat byproducts, meat and bone meal, and animal fat, which probably won't appeal to you but are nutritious and safe for your puppy. Higher quality foods usually have meat or meat products near the top of the ingredient list, but you don't need to worry about grain products as long as the label indicates that the food is nutritionally complete. Dogs are omnivores (not carnivores, as commonly believed), so all balanced dog foods contain animal and plant ingredients.

STAGES OF LIFE

When selecting your dog's diet, three stages of development must be considered: the puppy stage, the adult stage, and the senior stage.

Puppy Diets: Pups instinctively want to nurse, and a normal puppy will exhibit this behavior from just a few moments following birth. Puppies should be allowed to nurse for about the first six weeks, although from

Hypoglycemia (low blood sugar) is a potentially life-threatening problem of Yorkies and other toy breeds. The most common type of hypoglycemia occurs in puppies younger than four months of age. Puppies typically develop hypoglycemia after exercising vigorously, when they're stressed (such as during a trip to the veterinarian) or when they've gone too long without eating.

Toy breed puppies have various anatomical, physiological, and behavioral factors that contribute to the development of hypoglycemia: small muscle mass and liver (areas where glucose is stored as glycogen, a large molecule made up of many molecules of glucose linked together); proportionately large brain (a major user of glucose); and high activity level. Immaturity of the body's systems for processing and storing glucose may also play a role.

Early symptoms—trembling, listlessness, incoordination, and a dazed or confused demeanor—occur when the brain is deprived of glucose, its sole energy supply. If untreated, hypoglycemia can lead to seizures, collapse, loss of consciousness, and death.

If your Yorkie develops symptoms of hypoglycemia, start treatment immediately. Wrap your little buddy in a towel or blanket to keep him warm (shivering makes the hypoglycemia worse). If your Yorkie is conscious, slowly dribble a little corn syrup or honey into his mouth or give him a dollop of high-calorie dietary-supplement paste (available from your veterinarian). Repeat after ten minutes, if necessary.

Feed your Yorkie puppy as soon as he's alert enough to eat. If hypoglycemia causes your Yorkie to lose consciousness, rub the syrup or paste on her gums and tongue, then immediately take your pal to the veterinarian for further care.

If your puppy is prone to developing hypoglycemia, you should feed her a high-quality nutritionally balanced food four to five times a day.

Healthy high-calorie snacks may help prevent hypoglycemia between meals. If possible, avoid subjecting your Yorkie puppy to circumstances that may elicit hypoglycemia, such as stressful situations or extended periods of vigorous activity. Most puppies outgrow hypoglycemia by the time they're four months old. Consult your veterinarian if your Yorkie continues to have hypoglycemic episodes after this age.

the third or fourth week, the breeder will begin to introduce small portions of suitable solid food. Most breeders like to introduce alternate milk and meat meals initially, building up to weaning time.

By the time the puppies are seven or a maximum of eight weeks old, they should be fully weaned and fed solely on a proprietary puppy food. Selection of the most suitable, good-quality diet at this time is essential, for a puppy's fastest growth rate is during the first year of life. Seek advice about your dog's food from your veterinarian. The frequency of meals will be reduced over time, and when a young dog has reached the age of about ten to twelve months, he should be switched to an adult diet.

Puppy and junior diets can be well bal-anced for the needs of your Yorkshire Terrier so that, except in certain circumstances, additional vitamins, minerals, and proteins will not be required.

How many times a day does your Yorkie need to eat? Puppies—especially toy breeds—have small stomachs and high metabolic rates, so they need to eat several times a day in order to consume sufficient nutrients. If your puppy is younger than three months old, feed him four or five meals a day. When your little buddy is three to five months old, decrease the number of meals to three or four. At six months of age, most puppies can move to an adult schedule of two meals a day. If your Yorkie is prone to hypoglycemia (low blood sugar), a veterinarian may recommend more frequent meals.

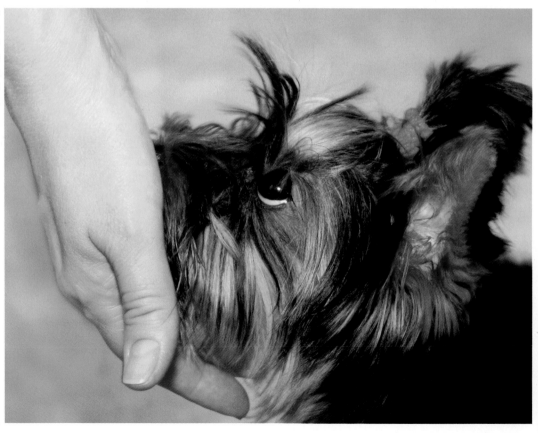

Spoil your Yorkie with healthy treats like those on the next page.

These delicious, dog-friendly recipes will have your furry friend smacking his lips and salivating for more. Just remember: Treats aren't meant to replace your dog's regular meals. Give your Yorkie snacks sparingly and continue to feed him nutritious, well-balanced meals.

Cheddar Squares

$\frac{1}{3}$ cup all-natural applesauce
$\frac{1}{3}$ cup low-fat cheddar cheese, shredded
$\frac{1}{3}$ cup water
2 cups unbleached white flour

In a medium bowl, mix all wet ingredients. In a large bowl, mix all dry ingredients. Slowly add the wet ingredients to the dry mixture. Mix well. Pour batter into a greased 13x9x2-inch pan. Bake at 375-degrees Fahrenheit for 25 to 30 minutes. Bars are done when a toothpick inserted in the center and removed comes out clean. Cool and cut into bars. Makes about 54 one-and-a-half-inch bars.

Peanut Butter Bites

3 tablespoons vegetable oil
$\frac{1}{4}$ cup smooth peanut butter, no salt or sugar
$\frac{1}{4}$ cup honey
1 $\frac{1}{2}$ teaspoon baking powder
2 eggs
2 cups whole wheat flower

In a large bowl, mix all ingredients until dough is firm. If the dough is too sticky, mix in a small amount of flour. Knead dough on a lightly floured surface until firm. Roll out dough half an inch thick and cut with cookie cutters. Put cookies on a cookie sheet half an inch apart. Bake at 350-degrees Fahrenheit for 20 to 25 minutes. When done, cookies should be firm to the touch. Turn oven off and leave cookies for one to two hours to harden. Makes about 40 two-inch-long cookies.

Adult Diets: A dog is considered an adult when he has stopped growing, so in general, the diet of a Yorkie can be changed to an adult one at about nine to twelve months of age. Again, rely upon your veterinarian or dietary specialist to recommend an acceptable maintenance diet. Major dog food manufacturers specialize in this type of food, and smart owners must select the one best suited to his needs. Do not leave food out all day for "free-choice" feeding, as this freedom inevitably translates to inches around the dog's waist.

Senior Diets: As dogs get older, their metabolism changes. The older dog usually exercises less, moves more slowly and sleeps more. This change in lifestyle and physiological performance requires a change in diet. Because these changes take place slowly, they might not be recognizable.

These metabolic changes increase the tendency toward obesity, requiring an even more vigilant approach to feeding. Obesity in an older dog compounds the health problems that already accompany old age.

As your Yorkie gets older, few of his organs function up to par. The kidneys slow down, and the intestines become less efficient. These age-related factors are best handled with a change in diet and a change in feeding schedule to give smaller portions that are more easily digested.

There is no single best diet for every older dog. While many dogs do well on light or senior diets, other dogs do better on a special premium diets such as lamb and rice. Be sensitive to your senior Yorkie's diet, and this will help control other problems that may arise with your old friend.

They may be small, but Yorkies do enjoy eating. Be sure to keep in mind that a little dog doesn't need many extra calories to become overweight.

The ideal Yorkshire Terrier coat is often described as silky, and it combs and brushes much like your own hair. However, just as most humans don't have hair that resembles the models in shampoo commercials, many Yorkies don't have the true silky coat. Instead, they have a soft coat. The grooming needs of the silky and soft coat types can be somewhat different. Take a moment to assess the type of hair your pet has. Does it lie close to the body, sleekly descending down the ribcage? Or is it fluffier, with more texture? The soft, fluffy coat has a tendency to tangle easily, so it requires diligent brushing. If neglected, the silky hair will also snag.

TOOLS OF THE TRADE

The correct tools will make your grooming much simpler, so take a list to your local pet-supply store and pick up these items:

Pin brush: This handled brush has straight metal pins set into soft rubber. The rubber that the pins are set in gives so as you brush your Yorkie you aren't as likely to hurt his skin. Slicker brushes, with bent metal teeth that catch mats or tangles, can break off

Did You Know? Nail clipping can be tricky, so many dog owners leave the task for the professionals. However, if you walk your dog on concrete, you may not have to worry about it. The concrete acts like a nail file and will probably keep the nails short and smooth.

in the coat. Most pet owners aren't concerned about coat breakage the way show-dog owners are. Desiring a quicker method of brushing, many pet owners choose the slicker brush because it can detangle the coat faster than a pin brush. Depending on how thorough your grooming routine becomes, you may need both types of brushes.

Combs: Most groomers use a metal dual-sided comb that has both close-set and wide-spaced teeth. Another choice is a rat-tailed comb, which has a long, thin handle (available at beauty-supply stores) and is helpful in setting the part down the middle of the back.

Premium dog shampoo and conditioner: Do not use human shampoo on your dog. Canine and human skin have different pH chemistry, so the shampoos are not interchangeable.

Small, latex hair bands: If you are going to comb your Yorkie's hair into a top-knot, do not reach for rubber bands—they quickly mat in the coat and cause breakage. Latex bands can be found at beauty-supply stores and at the orthodontist (people use them for their braces).

Child's soft toothbrush: Use this to clean the dog's face during his bath.

Ear cleaner and powder: Yorkshire Terriers must have the hair plucked from inside their ears because excessive hair growth in the ear collects wax and debris. Powder—applied to your fingers—will help you grasp and pull the hair.

Nail clippers and styptic powder: There are several kinds of nail clippers. Handle each kind in your hand to decide which model you prefer to use. It's purely a personal preference whether to use the guillotine or the scissor-action type.

Toothbrush and doggie toothpaste: Brushing your dog's teeth is a must. Buy the yummy doggie toothpaste with flavors your dog will like. Human toothpaste has a soap component that should not be swallowed, and doggie toothpaste has an abrasive component. We spit out our toothpaste, but dogs can't do the same, so they need digestible toothpaste.

Detangling spray: Many products help control static electricity, which is generated when you brush your Yorkie's coat.

Load up on dog-friendly tools to groom your Yorkie.

Control static with a spray that will keep your Yorkie's coat silky smooth.

NOTABLE & QUOTABLE

After removing a tick, clean the dog's skin with hydrogen peroxide. If Lyme disease is common where you live, have your veterinarian test the tick. Tick preventive medication will discourage ticks from attaching and kill any that do.

—groomer Andrea Vilardi from West Paterson, N.J.

A Yorkie's signature accessory is a little bow.

Small electric clipper: You can find these at beauty-supply stores and they're relatively inexpensive. Clippers come in handy for touch-up grooming and for sanitary reasons, such as shaving the hair around the rectum and genital areas to keep them clean.

BRUSHING LINE BY LINE

The interesting fact about a Yorkshire Terrier's coat is that it perpetually grows. It doesn't hit one length and stop growing, which is why you see Yorkies at dog shows with long, flowing coats that gracefully swing from side to side as they run. The same coat that breeders strive to produce can be the bane of a Yorkie owner's existence. You love your Yorkie for his temperament, great personality, and his beauty. However, keeping your dog in a full, beautiful coat requires dedication and commitment to a regular grooming routine.

Learn a brushing technique called "line brushing" to facilitate coat maintenance. Training your dog to lie down on his side makes the job much easier. Using one hand, push the hair from the ribcage up and over the body, then hold that hair in place.

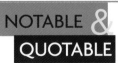

NOTABLE & QUOTABLE

Nail clipping is about the worst. And some of them don't like being groomed, period. But not too many—Yorkshire Terriers usually like the attention.

— *Mary Kesterson, a professional groomer and Yorkie breeder based in Tucson, Az.*

Yorkies with untrimmed hair need dedicated owners.

Holding your brush in the other hand, begin to section off about a half inch of hair in a horizontal line, and move up the body brushing only a small amount of hair with each increment. Use long straight strokes, from the skin to the ends of the coat. It sounds trickier than it is, but with a little practice, it will make brushing your Yorkie much easier.

Brush that same segment with a comb. If you hit a tangle, separate it with your fingers and brush it completely out. Then just switch sides. Brush the face and topknot and replace the bands in the top-knot each day so it doesn't become tangled in the hair. Avoid using rubber bands in place of latex—they cause hair breakage and may tangle in the hair to the point of needing to be cut out.

Be firm while training your Yorkie to be groomed, and do not allow him to bite the brush (or you). Use treats as enticements and rewards if you need to. Brushing should not be a chore; your dog should enjoy the attention.

JOIN OUR ONLINE Club Yorkie®

Every Yorkshire Terrier should look terrific. What do you need to keep your dog looking his best? Go to Club Yorkie (**DogChannel.com/Club-Yorkie**) and download a checklist of essential grooming equipment you and your Yorkie will need.

BATHING BASICS

The key to a successful Yorkie bath is organization. Keep all your grooming tools in a basket so you can prepare for the bath in only a moment. (This comes in handy when your zestful Yorkie finds something interesting in the yard to roll in, and you need to move quickly!) Some Yorkshire Terrier owners bathe their dogs in the kitchen sink because it's easier than kneeling over the bathtub. A hose attachment works well to saturate the coat.

You might try a restraining device, which is available in pet-supply stores. One style has a suction cup that attaches to the side of the tub or sink, and a loop that slides over the head and one front leg. The dog is controlled, and the loop is not in danger of choking your dog's slender neck.

Check the temperature and the pressure of the water against the inside of your wrist

SMART TIP!

Regular grooming is a required part of your dog's life. Realize that you can never, ever leave a Yorkie unattended on a table, or in the tub. He will jump!

or with your hand. Hold the hose close to your dog's body to eliminate excessive spray. If you don't have a hose attachment, use a plastic cup to scoop water and pour it over the dog.

Never bathe a matted or tangled dog; the mats will only shrink, worsen, and become that much more difficult to remove. Thoroughly brush your dog prior to his bath, then use a squeezing motion or a bristle or curry brush to distribute the shampoo throughout the coat. A back and forth massaging action can retangle the coat. Distribute the shampoo in the same manner you brush the coat—in long, sweeping motions.

Work from the highest point of your dog to the lowest, using your fingers to work the shampoo throughout the coat. For the face, use a child's soft toothbrush to clean the mustache and around the eye area and beard. The bristles are soft, but stiff enough to distribute the shampoo.

To keep water from getting into the nose when you rinse this area, hold your hand as a barrier around the nose, and let the water flow from behind the ears toward your hand and sort of break against the hand, descending over the beard.

Rinse your Yorkie with a gentle flow of water until the hair feels clean and the water runs clear. Use coat conditioners or a detangling solution after a bath, but use sparingly so as not to clog the pores. Follow the instructions on the bottle.

When drying the coat, use a blotting technique, squeezing the hair instead of rubbing the towel back and forth, to prevent matting. If you use a hair dryer, test the air flow against the inside of your wrist first, then hold it about ten to twelve inches from the dog.

Do not move the air back and forth (this will tangle the coat). Instead, focus on one small area at a time and blow the hair in one direction. If you're using a grooming table with a restraining device, point the dryer at the coat with one hand and brush with the other while the dog is drying.

Remember, it's never safe to walk away from your dog, either when he's on a table or in the bathtub. Remain with the dog until it's time to pick him up and set him on the floor. Allowing your dog to jump from the tub or table when bath time is over is also a big no-no because your dog can injure himself.

FOUR STEPS TO TYING A TOPKNOT

Tying a topknot on your Yorkie will take some practice.

Step One: Part the hair from the corner of both eyes to just behind the dimple behind

Use a soft hand towel to gently clean your Yorkie's face.

each eye on the skull. Gather that hair and comb it forward. Attach a latex band to this hair making sure you don't gather the hair too tightly. Try to leave about an inch between the band and the skin. The topknot should be in the center of the head, close to the eyes.

Step Two: Separate the topknot horizontally into a front section and a back section, then divide the back section in half again—front to back. Take the two back sections and pull evenly on them, this forms the "bubble" in the front part of the topknot. Slide the bow on over the first band.

Step Three: For the correct Yorkshire topknot, you will need to make a second topknot behind the front one. (A simpler version with just one topknot can also be done.) Part the hair on each side to behind the occipital (the large bone on top of the head). Connect

the two side parts behind the occipital bone in a V-shape. Comb that hair forward and put a band on it. Divide that topknot from front to back. Lightly pull on the front of the rear topknot to move it closer to the finished topknot in front.

Step Four: To keep the topknot neat and make it easier to wrap a band around it, the hair is gathered into a thick strand and folded into a loop. Comb both topknots together and fold the strand into a short loop so the end of the topknot hair hangs behind and to the side; anchor them together with a band, or with your ribbon. The long hair should hang to the rear and off to the side of the topknot.

ABOUT THE PUPPY CUT

Many dog owners ask their groomers to make their dog look "like a puppy again." Yorkshire Terrier puppies are darling with their fluffy, short, dark hair, and bristly face, and your adult Yorkie can have this look again with a puppy cut. The puppy cut gives an adult Yorkie a short, fluffy coat that resembles his younger days. The idea is to give the dog a cute, cuddly look that is also easy to maintain.

The problem with executing this clip comes from the texture of the hair. Yorkie coats are divided into two types. The show coat, which is silky, often looks hacked when shortened. The soft coat cuts better and will hold a short style. Ask your groomer if a puppy cut is right for your Yorkie.

So, where are you going to find the person to give this darling cut to your Yorkie?

Good groomers are known for their skill and reputation. Ask your friends and your veterinarian to recommend someone they would be comfortable entrusting with your dog. Once you have several referrals, call and request a tour of their shops, at their convenience, of course. Most groomers won't allow strangers access while their shop is filled with clients' dogs, some of which might bite; however, they should be willing to show you around either prior to opening or after closing.

Have a list of questions to ask groomers about their business practices. Find out whether they hand dry or cage dry the dogs; what type of shampoos they use; and how long you can expect the dog to be at the groomers. Some shops are like hair salons, and each dog is worked on by one person from start to finish. Others work more like an assembly line, with dogs in different stages of completion.

While you are there, go ahead and give the shop the sniff test. Take a big, deep breath. A clean shop will not smell like a herd of dirty dogs; it will smell like whatever shampoo or colognes being used. Take the time to look around. Clean shops sweep as they go. As each dog is finished, the groomer cleans and sanitizes the table and equipment, then sweeps up the hair. Also check to see if the groomer has any professional certification, such as Certified

Master Groomer. With a little work, you can find a groomer to care for your pet from puppyhood to old age, or from puppy cut to show coat.

NOW HEAR THIS!

While you're in the process of washing your Yorkie, gently wipe the inside of the ears with a damp face cloth. The ears should be kept clean and any excess hair inside the ear should be carefully plucked out. Take a commercial ear cleaner and place a few drops in each ear canal. Most dogs shake their heads when you do this. Have a towel handy to block the escaping solution. Never force your finger or any object down into the deeper part of the ear. Wipe only the surface you can see and touch easily. Any further cleaning must be performed by your vet.

it's a Fact Yorkie puppies aren't born with the trademark Yorkshire Terrier coat. They're born with a softer, shorter, black-and-tan coat. As they mature, they develop their long, smooth, blue-and-tan coat.

Ask the groomer if a puppy cut is the right cut for your Yorkie.

Be on the lookout for any signs of infection or ear-mite infestation. If your Yorkshire Terrier has been shaking his head or scratching at his ears frequently, this usually indicates a problem. If your Yorkie's ears have an unusual odor, this is a sure sign of mite infestation or infection, and a signal to have his ears checked by your veterinarian.

CUT THOSE NAILS

You should trim your Yorkie's nails every two to three weeks. Periodic nail trimming can be done during the brushing routine. Your veterinarian will teach you how to cut your dog's nails without cutting the "quick" (the blood vessels that run through the center of each nail and grow rather close to the end).

It takes a lot of effort to primp a Yorkie, so find a groomer who knows how to handle these darling divas.

Your Yorkie should be accustomed to having his nails trimmed at an early age because it will be part of your maintenance routine throughout his life. Not only do neatly trimmed nails look nicer, but long nails can scratch someone unintentionally. Also, a long nail has a better chance of ripping and bleeding, or causing the feet to spread. A good rule of thumb is that if you can hear your dog's nails' clicking on the floor when he walks, his nails are too long.

Before you start cutting, make sure you can identify the "quick" in each nail. It will bleed if accidentally cut, which will be quite painful for the dog because it contains nerve endings. Keep some type of clotting agent on hand, such as a styptic pencil or styptic powder (the type used for shaving). This will stop the bleeding

quickly when applied to the end of the cut nail. Do not panic if this happens, just stop the bleeding and talk soothingly to your dog. Once he has calmed down, move on to the next nail. It is better to clip a little at a time, particularly with black-nailed dogs.

Hold your Yorkie puppy steady as you begin trimming his nails; you don't want him to make any sudden movements or run away. Talk to him soothingly and stroke him as you clip. Holding his foot in your hand, simply take off the end of each nail in one quick clip. You can purchase nail clippers that are specially made for dogs; which you can find wherever you buy grooming supplies.

There are two predominant types of clippers. One is the guillotine clipper, which is a hole with a blade in the middle. Squeeze the handles, and the blade meets the nail and chops it off. Sounds gruesome, and for some dogs, it is intolerable. Scissor-type clippers are gentler on the nail. The important thing to make sure of is that the blades on either of these clippers are sharp.

Once you are at the desired length, use a nail file to smooth the rough edges of the nails so they don't catch on carpeting or debris outdoors.

it's a Fact Dogs can't rinse and spit after brushing, so dog toothpaste must be safe for pets to swallow. Always use a toothpaste specially formulated for dogs when brushing your Yorkie's teeth.

EXTRA TRIMMINGS

Clip the hair near the pads of the feet with an electric trimmer. This keeps your Yorkie's braking system working and keeps him from sliding on slippery floors. Using a very light touch, trim the hair around the rectal area to prevent feces from adhering to the hair. Keep the blade pointing horizontally to the dog's skin to minimize the likelihood of clipping the skin. Shave the top half of the ear from front to back to allow the hair to hang naturally. Unless the dog has a puppy cut (a style that keeps the coat shorter and more manageable), try to avoid trimming the hair around the nose, simply brush it down so it doesn't irritate the eyes.

After trimming and brushing, you'll need to set the part going down the center of the back along the spine. You can use the tail of a comb or a thin knitting needle to part the hair from the back of the head to the tailset. As the hair parts, brush it into place. A light spray of hairspray or coat conditioner will help to hold it.

TEETH TALK

Like people, Yorkies can suffer from dental disease, so experts recommend regular tooth brushing. Daily brushing is best, but your dog will benefit from tooth brushing a few times a week. The teeth should be white and free of yellowish tartar, and the gums should appear healthy and pink. Gums that bleed easily when you perform dental duties may have gingivitis.

The first thing to know is that your puppy probably isn't going to want your fingers in his mouth. Desensitizing your puppy—getting him to accept that you will be looking at and touching his teeth—is the first step to overcoming his reticence. You can begin this as soon as you get your puppy, with the help of the thing that motivates him most: food.

If your Yorkie likes to let the wind blow through his fur, be sure to use a de-tangling spray.

For starters, let your Yorkie lick some chicken, vegetable or beef broth off your finger. Then, dip your finger in broth again, and gently insert your finger in the side of your dog's mouth. Touch his side teeth and gums. Several sessions will get your puppy used to having his mouth touched.

Use a toothbrush specifically made for a dog or a finger-tip brush to brush your Yorkie's teeth. Hold the mouth with the fingers of one hand, and brush with the other. Use toothpaste made specifically for dogs with dog-slurping flavors like poultry and beef. The human kind froths too much and can give your dog an upset stomach. Brush in a circular motion with the brush held at a forty-five-degree angle to the gum line. Be sure to get the fronts, tops, and sides of each tooth.

Look for signs of plaque, tartar or gum disease, including redness, swelling, foul breath, discolored enamel near the gumline, and receding gums. If you see these, take your dog to the veterinarian immediately. Also see your vet about once a year for a dental checkup.

TRAIN

It's easy to fall into the trap of thinking your Yorkie doesn't need training. He's so little, it's no big deal to pick him up when you need to take him somewhere. But if you want him to be a mentally and physically healthy, well-adjusted member of society instead of a snappy little arm-shark, some basic training is in order. Whatever your goals for your relationship with your pint-sized pal, they'll be best achieved if you take the time to teach your Yorkie a solid foundation of good manners.

Reward-based training methods—clicker and luring—show dogs what to do and help them do it correctly, setting them up for success and rewards rather than mistakes and punishment. Most dogs find food rewards meaningful; Yorkies are no exception. They tend to be very food-motivated.

This works well because positive training relies on using treats, at least initially, to encourage the dog to demonstrate a behavior. The treat is then given as a reward. When you reinforce desired behaviors with rewards that are valuable to the dog, you are met with happy cooperation rather than resistance.

Did You Know?

The prime period for socialization is short. Most behavior experts agree that positive experiences during the ten-week period between four and fourteen weeks of age are vital to the development of a puppy who'll grow into an adult dog with sound temperament.

Positive reinforcement does not mean permissive. While you are rewarding your Yorkshire Terrier's desirable behaviors, you must manage him to be sure he doesn't get rewarded for his undesirable behaviors. Training tools, such as leashes, tethers, baby gates, and crates, help keep your dog out of trouble, and the use of force-free negative punishment (the dog's behavior makes a good thing go away) helps him realize there are negative consequences for inappropriate behaviors.

LEARNING SOCIAL GRACES

Now that you have done all of the preparatory work and have helped your Yorkie get accustomed to his new home and family, it is time for you to have some fun! Socializing your tiny pup gives you the opportunity to show off your new friend, and your Yorkie gets to reap the benefits of being an adorable little creature that people will want to pet and, in general, think is absolutely precious!

Besides getting to know his new family, your puppy should be exposed to other people, animals and situations, but of course he must not come into close contact with dogs you don't know well until he has had all his vaccinations. This will help him become well adjusted as he grows up and less prone to being timid or fearful of the new things he will encounter.

Your pup's socialization began at the breeder's home, but now it is your responsi-

Don't forget to incorporate treats into training!

bility to continue it. The socialization he receives up until the age of twelve weeks is the most critical, as this is the time when he forms his impressions of the outside world. Be especially careful during the eight- to ten-week period, also known as the fear period. The interaction he receives during this time should be gentle and reassuring. Lack of socialization can manifest itself in fear and aggression as the dog grows up. The pup needs lots of human contact, affection, handling, and exposure to other animals.

Once your Yorkshire Terrier has received his necessary vaccinations, feel free to take

NOTABLE & QUOTABLE

Yorkies are bright and quick learners, and they love to train. They are not little stuffed animals, and they deserve to be treated respectfully. Yorkies are full of fun, and thrive on love, attention, and training.

— *Tara McLaughlin, a certified pet dog trainer and Yorkie owner in Charlottesville, Va.*

him out and about (on his leash, of course). Walk him around the neighborhood, take him on your daily errands, let people pet him, let him meet other dogs and pets. Make sure to expose your Yorkie to different people—men, women, kids, babies, men with beards, teenagers with cell phones or riding skateboards, joggers, shoppers, someone in a wheelchair, a pregnant woman, etc. Make sure your Yorkie explores different surfaces like sidewalks, gravel, and a puddle. Positive experience is the key to building confidence. It's up to you to make sure your Yorkie safely discovers the world so he will be a calm, confident, and well-socialized dog.

It's very important that you take the lead in all socialization experiences and never put your puppy into a scary or potentially harmful situation. Be mindful of your Yorkie's limitations. Fifteen minutes at a public market is

SMART TIP!

If your Yorkie refuses to sit with both haunches squarely beneath him and instead sits on one side or the other, he may have a physical reason for doing so. Discuss the habit with your veterinarian to be certain that your dog isn't suffering from some structural problem.

fine; two hours at a loud outdoor concert is too much. Meeting vaccinated, tolerant and gentle older dogs is great. Meeting dogs that you don't know isn't a great idea, especially if they appear very energetic, dominant, or fearful. Control the situations in which you place your puppy.

The best way to socialize your puppy to a new experience is to make him think it's the best thing ever. You can do this with a lot of happy talk, enthusiasm, and, yes, food.

A mannered Yorkie is a delight to live with.

Yorkies and other pets should be introduced slowly and always watched closely.

To convince your puppy that almost any experience is a blast, always carry treats. Consider carrying two types—a bag of his puppy chow, which you can give him when introducing him to nonthreatening experi-ences, and a bag of high-value, mouth-watering treats to give him when introduc-ing him to scarier experiences.

BASIC CUES

All Yorkies, regardless of your training and relationship goals, need to know at least five basic good-manner behaviors: sit, down, stay, come, and heel. Here are tips for teach-ing your dog these important cues.

Sit: Every dog should learn how to sit.

▲ Hold a treat at the end of your Yorkshire Terrier's nose.

▲ Move the treat over his head.

▲ When he sits, click a clicker or say "Yes!"

▲ Feed your dog the treat.

▲ If your dog jumps up, hold the treat lower. If he backs up, back him into a corner and wait until he sits. Be patient. Keep your clicker handy, and click (or say "Yes!") and treat anytime he offers a sit.

▲ When he easily offers sits, say "sit" just before he offers, so he can make the association between the word and the behavior. Add the sit cue when you know you can get the behavior. Your dog doesn't know what the word means until you repeatedly associate it with the appropriate behavior.

▲ When your Yorkie sits easily on cue, start using intermittent reinforcement by clicking some sits but not others. At first, click most sits and skip an occasional one (this is a high rate of reinforcement). Gradually make your clicks more and more random.

Down: If your Yorkie can sit, then he can learn to lie down.

▼ Have your Yorkshire Terrier sit.

▼ Hold the treat in front of his nose. Move it down slowly, straight toward the floor (toward his toes). If he follows all the way down, click and treat.

▼ If he gets stuck, move the treat down more slowly. Click and treat for small movements downward—moving his head a bit lower, or inching one paw forward. Keep clicking and treating until your Yorkie is all the way down. This is called "shaping"—rewarding small pieces of a behavior until your dog succeeds.

▼ If your dog stands as you move the treat toward the floor, have him sit, and move the treat more slowly downward, shaping with clicks and treats for small movement down as long as he is sitting. If he stands, cheerfully say "Oops!" (which means "Sorry, no treat for

that!"), have him sit, and try again.

▼ If shaping isn't working, sit on the floor with your knee raised. Have your Yorkie sit next to you. Put your hand with the treat under your knee and lure him under your leg so that he lies down and crawls to follow the treat. Click and treat!

▼ When you can lure the down easily, add the verbal cue, wait a few seconds to let your dog think, then lure him down to show him the association. Repeat until he'll go down on the verbal cue. Then begin using intermittent reinforcement.

Stay: What good are sit and down cues if your dog doesn't stay?

● Start with your Yorkshire Terrier in a sit or down position.

JOIN OUR ONLINE
Club Yorkie®

With the proper training, your Yorkie will be as well behaved as he is adorable. One certification that all dogs should receive is the American Kennel Club Canine Good Citizen that rewards dogs with good manners. Go to **DogChannel.com/Club-Yorkie** and click on "downloads" to get the ten steps required for your dog to be a CGC.

At minimum, your Yorkie should learn the five basic cues: sit, stay, lie down, come, and heel.

● Put the treat in front of your dog's nose and keep it there.

● Click and reward several times while he is in position, then release him with a cue that you will always use to tell him the stay is over. Common release cues are: "all done," "break," "free," "free dog," "at ease," and "OK."

● When your Yorkshire Terrier will stay in sit or down position while you click and treat, add your verbal stay cue. Say "stay," pause for a second or two, click and say "stay" again. Release.

● When he's getting the idea, say "stay," whisk the treat out of sight behind your back, click, and whisk the treat back. Be sure to get it all the way to his nose, so he doesn't jump up. Gradually increase the duration of the stay.

● When your Yorkie will stay for fifteen to twenty seconds, add small distractions: shuffling your feet, moving your arms, small hops. Increase distractions gradually.

Did You Know?

Once your Yorkie understands what behavior goes with a specific cue, it is time to start weaning him off the food treats. At first, give a treat after each exercise. Then, start to give a treat only after every other exercise. Mix up the times when you offer a food reward and when you only offer praise. This way your dog will never know when he is going to receive food and praise or only praise.

If he makes mistakes, you're adding too much, too fast.

● When he'll stay for fifteen to twenty seconds with distractions, gradually add distance. Have your dog stay, take a half-step back, click, return, and treat. When he'll stay with a half-step, tell him to stay, take a full step back, click, and return. Always return to your dog to treat after you click, but before you release. If you always return, his stay becomes strong. If you call him to you, his stay gets weaker due to his eagerness to come to you.

Come: A reliable recall—coming when called—can be a challenging behavior to teach. It is possible, however. To succeed, you need to install an automatic response to your "come" cue—one so automatic that your Yorkie doesn't even stop to think when he hears it, but will spin on his heels and charge to you at full speed.

■ Start by charging a come cue the same way you charged your clicker. If your Yorkie already ignores the word "come," pick a different cue, like "front" or "hugs." Say your cue and feed him a bit of scrumptious treat. Repeat this until his eyes light up when he hears the cue. Now you're ready to start training.

■ With your Yorkie on a leash, run away several steps and cheerfully call out your charged cue. When he follows, click the clicker. Feed him a treat when he reaches you. For a more enthusiastic come, run away at full speed as you call him. When he follows at a gallop, click, stop running, and give him a treat. The better your Yorkie gets at coming, the farther away he can be when you call him.

■ Once your Yorkshire Terrier understands the come cue, play with more people, each with a clicker and treats. Stand a short distance apart and take turns calling

SMART TIP!

If you begin teaching the heel cue by taking long walks and letting the dog pull you along, he may misinterpret this action as an acceptable form of taking a walk. When you pull back on the leash to counteract his pulling, he will read that tug as a signal to pull even harder!

Once your dog learns the basics, you can begin to teach him more complicated cues and tricks.

and running away. Click and treat in turn as he comes to each of you. Gradually increase the distance until he comes flying to each person from a distance.

■ When you and your Yorkshire Terrier are ready to practice in wide-open spaces, attach a long line—a 20- to 50-foot leash—to your dog, so you can gather up your

They may look like little angels, but Yorkies are often the instigators of dog fights. Despite their size, they rarely back down, and dog fights—and serious injuries—can happen in a flash. Puppies can begin displaying defensive behavior like growling, snapping, or lunging at other dogs as young as four months of age. It should never be ignored or encouraged. Respond quickly, calmly, and firmly to stop it or it's likely to intensify, and little dogs can get themselves into very big trouble this way.

Yorkie if that taunting squirrel nearby is too much of a temptation. Then head to a practice area where there are less tempting distractions.

Heel: Heeling means that the dog walks beside his owner without pulling. It takes time and patience on your part to succeed at teaching the dog that you will not proceed unless he is walking calmly beside him. Pulling out ahead on the leash is definitely not acceptable.

▲ Begin by holding the leash in your left hand as your Yorkie sits beside your left leg. Move the loop end of the leash to your right hand, but keep your left hand short on the leash so that it keeps the dog close to you.

▲ Say "heel" and step forward on your left foot. Keep your Yorkie close to you and take three steps. Stop and have the dog sit next to you in what we now call the heel position. Praise verbally, but do not touch the dog. Hesitate a moment and begin again with "heel," taking three steps and stopping, at which point the dog is told to sit again.

Never underestimate a Yorkie. Some puppies are not so busy and inquisitive, but not this breed. Their wheels are always turning, and they are always thinking about what they can get in next. It makes them fun but also makes them a challenge.

—Sharon Jones, a breeder in Mohrsville, Pa.

▲ Your goal here is to have your dog walk those three steps without pulling on the leash. Once he will walk calmly beside you for three steps without pulling, increase the number of steps you take to five. When he will walk politely beside you while you take five steps, you can increase the length of your walk to ten steps. Keep increasing the length of your stroll until the dog will walk quietly beside you without pulling for as long as you want him to heel. When you stop heeling, indicate to the dog that the exercise is over by petting him and saying "OK, good dog." The "OK" is used as a release word, meaning that the exercise is finished, and the dog is free to relax.

▲ If you are dealing with a Yorkshire Terrier who insists on pulling you around, simply put on your brakes and stand your ground until your Yorkie realizes that the two of you are not going anywhere until he is beside you and moving at your pace, not his. It may take some time just standing there to convince the dog that you are the leader, and you will be the one to decide on the direction and speed of your travel.

▲ Each time the dog looks up at you or slows down to give a slack leash between the two of you, quietly praise him and say, "Good heel. Good dog." Eventually, your Yorkie will begin to respond, and within a few days he will be walking politely beside you without pulling on the leash. At first, the training sessions should be kept short and very positive; soon the dog will be able to walk nicely with you for increasingly longer distances. Remember to give the dog free time and the opportunity to run and play when you have finished heel practice.

TRAINING TIPS

If not properly socialized, managed, and trained, even well-bred Yorkies will exhibit undesirable behaviors such as jumping up, barking, chasing, chewing, and other destructive behaviors. You can prevent these annoying habits and help your Yorkie become the perfect dog you're hoping for by following some basic training and behavior guidelines.

■ **Be consistent.** Consistency is important, not just in relation to what you allow

SMART TIP!

It's a good idea to enroll in an obedience class if one is available in your area. Many cities have dog clubs that offer basic obedience training as well as preparatory classes for obedience competition. There are also local dog trainers who offer similar classes.

your Yorkie to do (get on the sofa, perhaps) and not do (jump up on people), but also in the verbal and body language cues you use with your dog and in his daily routine.

■ **Be gentle but firm.** Positive training methods are very popular. Properly applied, dog-friendly methods are wonderfully effective, creating canine-human relationships based on respect and cooperation.

■ **Manage behavior.** All living things repeat behaviors that are rewarded. Behaviors that aren't reinforced will go away.

■ **Provide adequate exercise.** A tired dog is a well-behaved dog. Many behavior problems can be avoided, others resolved, simply by providing your Yorkshire Terrier with enough exercise.

THE THREE-STEP PROGRAM

Perhaps it's too late to give your dog consistency, training, and management from the start. Maybe he came from a Yorkie rescue or a shelter, or you didn't realize the importance of these tenets when he was a pup. He already may have learned some bad behaviors. Perhaps they're even part of his genetic package. Many problems can be modified with ease using the following three-step process for changing an unwanted behavior.

Step No. 1: Visualize the behavior you want. If you simply try to stop your Yorkie from doing something, you leave a behavior vacuum. You need to fill that vacuum with something, so your dog doesn't return to the same behavior or fill it with one

that's even worse! If you're tired of your dog jumping up, decide what you'd prefer instead. A dog who greets people by sitting politely in front of them is a joy to own.

Step No. 2: Prevent your Yorkshire from being rewarded for the behavior you don't want. Management to the rescue! When your Yorkie jumps up to greet you or get your attention, turn your back and step away to show him that jumping up no longer works to gain attention.

Step No. 3: Generously reinforce the desired behavior. Remember, dogs repeat behaviors that reward them. If your Yorkie no longer gets attention for jumping up and is heavily reinforced with attention and treats for sitting, he will offer sits instead of jumping, because sits get him what he wants.

COUNTER CONDITIONING

Behaviors that respond well to the three-step process are those where the dog does something in order to get good stuff. He jumps up to get attention. He countersurfs because he finds good stuff on counters. He nips at your hands to get you to play with him.

The three steps don't work well when you're dealing with behaviors that are based in strong emotion, such as aggression and fear, or with hardwired behaviors such as chasing prey. With these, you can change the emotional or hardwired response through counter conditioning—programming a new emotional or automatic response to the stimulus by giving it a new association. Here's how you would counter condition a Yorkshire Terrier who chases after skateboarders when you're walking him on a leash.

Have a large supply of very high-value treats, such as canned chicken.

Try not to get frustrated if your Yorkie is just not getting it. With patience, he'll pick up the cues in time.

Station yourself with your Yorkie on a leash at a location where skateboarders will pass by at a subthreshold distance "X"—that is, where your Yorkie alerts but doesn't lunge and bark.

Wait for a skateboarder. The instant your Yorkie notices the skateboarder, feed him bits of chicken, nonstop, until the skateboarder is gone. Stop feeding him the chicken.

Repeat many times until, when the skateboarder appears, your Yorkie looks at you with a big grin as if to say, "Yay! Where's my chicken?" This is a conditioned emotional response, or CER.

When you have a consistent CER at X, decrease the distance slightly, perhaps minus 1 foot, and repeat until you consistently get the CER at this distance.

Continue decreasing the distance and obtaining a CER at each level, until a skateboarder zooming right past your Yorkshire Terrier elicits the happy "Where's my chicken?" response. Now go back to distance X and add a second zooming skateboarder. Continue this process of gradual desensitization until your Yorkshire Terrier doesn't turn a hair at a bevy of skateboarders.

BAD HABITS

Discipline—training one to act in accordance with rules—brings order to life. It is as simple as that. Without discipline, particularly in a group society, chaos reigns supreme, and the group will eventually perish. Humans and canines are social animals and need some form of discipline in order to function effectively. Dogs need discipline in their lives in order to understand how their pack (you and other family members) functions and how they must act in order to survive.

Luckily, puppies are little sponges, waiting to soak up whatever information they can, be it bad habits or good manners. Start training early, and you can control what behaviors go into your terrier.

The following behavioral problems are the ones which Yorkie owners most commonly encounter. Every dog is unique and every situation is unique. Because behavioral abnormalities are the leading reason for owners' abandoning their pets, we hope that you will make a valiant effort to solve your Yorkie's problems.

Did You Know?

Anxiety can make a dog really miserable. Living in a world with scary, vaporous monsters and suspected Yorkie-eaters roaming the streets has to be pretty nerve-wracking. The good news is that timid dogs are not doomed to be forever ruled by fear. Owners who understand the timid terrier's needs can help him build self-confidence and a more optimistic view of life.

NIP NIPPING

As puppies start to teethe, they feel the need to sink their teeth into anything—unfortunately, that includes your fingers, arms, hair, toes, whatever happens to be available. You may find this behavior cute for about the first five seconds—until you feel just how sharp those puppy teeth are. This is something you want to discourage immediately and consistently with a firm "No!" (or whatever number of firm commands it takes for your dog to understand that you mean business) and replace your finger with an appropriate chew toy.

STOP THAT WHINING

A Yorkie puppy will often cry, whine, whimper, howl, or make some type of commotion when he is left alone. This is basically his way of calling out for attention, of calling out to make sure that you know he is there and that you have not forgotten about him. He feels insecure when he is left alone; for example, when you are out of the house and he is in his crate, or when you are in another part of the house and he cannot see you. The noise he is making is an expression of the anxiety he feels at being alone, so he needs to be taught that being alone is OK. You are not actually training the dog to stop making noise, you are training him to feel comfortable when he is alone and removing the need to make the noise.

This is where the crate with a cozy blanket and a toy comes in handy. You want to know that your pup is safe when you are not there to supervise, and you know that he will be safe in his crate rather than roaming freely about the house. In order for your pup to stay in his crate without making a fuss, he needs to feel comfortable in his crate. On that note, it is extremely important that the crate is never used as a form of punishment, or your pup will have a negative association with the crate.

Accustom your Yorkie to his crate in short, gradually increasing intervals of time, maybe with a treat or toy, and stay in the room with him. If he cries or makes a fuss, do not go to him, but stay in his sight. Gradually, he will realize that staying in his crate is all right, and it will not be so traumatic for him to be in the crate when you are not around. You may want to leave the radio on softly when you leave the house; the sound of human voices can be comforting to him.

CHEW ON THIS

The national canine pastime is chewing! Every dog loves to sink his "canines" into a tasty bone, but most anything will do! Dogs need to chew to massage their gums, to make their new teeth feel better and to exer-

SMART TIP!

The golden rule of dog training is simple. For each "question" (cue), there is only one correct answer (reaction). One cue equals one reaction. Keep practicing the cue until the dog reacts correctly without hesitation. Be repetitive but not monotonous. Dogs get bored just as people do; a bored dog's attention will not be focused on the lesson.

cise their jaws. This is a natural behavior deeply imbedded in all things canine. Our role as smart owners is not to stop our dogs from chewing, but to redirect it to positive, chew-worthy objects. Be an informed owner and purchase proper chew toys for your Yorkie, like strong nylon bones. Be sure that the devices are safe and durable because your dog's safety is at risk.

The best solution for inappropriate chew-

Dogs love to chew, so give them toys that they can really sink their teeth into.

Yorkies respond best to patient, persistent training.

ing is prevention: That is, put your shoes, handbags, and other tasty objects in their proper places (out of the reach of the growing canine mouth). Direct puppies to their toys whenever you see them tasting the furniture legs or the leg of your pants. Make a loud noise to attract your pup's attention, and immediately escort him to his chew toy and engage him with the toy for at least four minutes, praising and encouraging him.

NO MORE JUMPING

Jumping up is a dog's friendly way of saying hello, and some energetic Yorkies may get in this habit. Some dog owners do not mind when their dog jumps on them,

Did You Know?

Some natural remedies for separation anxiety are reputed to have calming effects, but check with your vet before use. Flower essence remedies are water-based extracts of different plants, which are stabilized and preserved with brandy. A human dose is only a few drops, so seek advice from a natural healing practitioner on proper dosage for your Yorkshire Terrier.

Your Yorkie may howl, whine, or otherwise vocalize his displeasure at your leaving the house and his being left alone. This is a normal case of separation anxiety, but there are things that can be done to eliminate this problem. Your dog needs to learn that he will be fine on his own for a while, and that he will not wither away if he is not attended to every minute of the day.

In fact, constant attention can lead to separation anxiety in the first place. If you are endlessly coddling and cuddling your dog, he will come to expect this from you all of the time and it will be more traumatic for him when you are not there.

To help minimize separation anxiety, make your entrances and exits as low-key as possible. Do not give your dog a long, drawn-out goodbye, and do not lavish him with hugs and kisses when you return. This will only make him miss it more when you are away. Another thing you can try is to give your dog a treat when you leave; this will keep him occupied, keep his mind off the fact that you just left, and help him associate your leaving with a pleasant experience.

You may have to accustom your dog to being left alone in intervals, much like when you introduced your pup to his crate. Of course, when your dog starts whimpering as you approach the door, your first instinct will be to run to him and comfort him, but don't do it! Eventually he will adjust and be just fine if you take it in small steps. His anxiety stems from being placed in an unfamiliar situation; by familiarizing him with being alone he will learn that he is OK.

When your dog is alone in the house, confine him in his crate or a designated dog-proof area of the house. This should be the area in which he sleeps, so he should already feel comfortable there and this should make him feel more at ease when he is alone. This is just one of the many examples in which a crate is an invaluable tool for you and your Yorkshire Terrier, and another reinforcement of why your dog should view his crate as a happy place, a place of his own.

Do not carry your dog to his relief area. Lead him there on a leash or, better yet, encourage him to follow you to the spot. If you start carrying him, you might end up doing this routine forever, and your dog will have the satisfaction of having trained you.

but the problem arises when guests come to the house and the dog greets them in the same manner—whether they like it or not! However friendly the greeting may be, chances are that some visitors will not appreciate being jumped on even by a tiny Yorkshire Terrier. The dog will not be able to distinguish whom he can jump on and whom he cannot. It is best to discourage this behavior entirely from a young age.

Pick a command such as "Off!" (avoid using "down" because you will use that for the dog to lie down) and tell him "Off!" when he jumps up. Place him on the ground on all fours and have him sit, praising him the whole time. Always lavish him with praise and petting when he is in the "sit" position. That way you are still giving your Yorkie a warm, affectionate greeting because you are as excited to see him as he is to see you!

UNWANTED BARKING MUST GO

Barking is a dog's way of talking, and little dogs like Yorkies always seem to have something to say. It can be somewhat frustrating because it is not easy to tell what your dog means by his bark: Is he excited, happy, frightened, angry? Whatever it is

Jumping up is your Yorkie's way of greeting you, but it should be discouraged to prevent bad behavior.

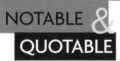

NOTABLE &
QUOTABLE

Stage false departures. Pick up your car keys and put on your coat, then put them away and go about your routine. Do this several times a day, ignoring your dog while you do it. Soon his reaction to these triggers will decrease.

— *September Morn, a dog trainer and behavior specialist in Bellingham, Wash.*

that the dog is trying to say, he should not be punished for barking. It is only when the barking becomes excessive, and when the excessive barking becomes a bad habit, that the behavior needs to be modified.

If an intruder came into your home in the middle of the night, and your Yorkie barked a warning, wouldn't you be pleased? You would probably deem your dog a hero, a wonderful guardian and protector of the home. On the other hand, if a friend drops by unexpectedly, rings the doorbell and is greeted with a sudden,

sharp bark, you would probably be annoyed at the dog. But isn't it just the same behavior? Your Yorkie doesn't know any better—unless he sees who is at the door and it is someone he is familiar with, he will bark as a means of vocalizing that his (and your) territory is being threatened. While your friend is not posing a threat, it is all the same to your dog. Barking is his means of letting you know that there is an intrusion, whether friend or foe, on your property. This type of barking is instinctive and should not be discouraged.

Excessive habitual barking, however, is a problem that should be corrected early on. As your Yorkie grows up, you will be able to tell when his barking is purposeful and when it is for no reason. You will become able to distinguish your dog's different barks and with what they are associated. For example, the bark when someone comes to the door will be different from the bark when he is excited to see you. It is similar to a person's tone of voice, except that the dog has to rely totally on tone of voice because he does not have the benefit of using words. An incessant barker will be evident at an early age.

There are some things that encourage a dog to bark. For example, if your dog barks nonstop for a few minutes and you give him a treat to quiet him, he believes that you are rewarding him for barking. He will associate

Barking is a way of life with dogs, but excessive barking should be banned.

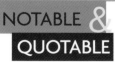
I warn all my owners that if they don't train the dog, the dog will train them! Yorkies have a bad reputation because their owners let them get away with spoiled child behavior.

—*breeder Sandy Fetchko from Chemainus, British Columbia, Canada*

barking with getting a treat, and he will keep doing it until he is rewarded.

STOP FOOD STEALING AND BEGGING

Is your dog devising ways of stealing food from your cupboards? If so, you must answer the following questions: Is your Yorkie hungry, or is he constantly famished? Why is there food on the coffee table? Face it, some dogs are more food-motivated than others; some dogs are totally obsessed by a slab of brisket and can only think of their next meal. Food stealing is terrific fun for a dog and always yields a great reward—food, glorious food!

A smart owner's goal, therefore, is to make the "reward" less rewarding, even startling! Plant a shaker can (an empty can with coins inside) on the table so that it catches your pooch off-guard. There are other devices available that will surprise your dog when he is looking for a midafternoon snack. Such remote-control devices, though not the first choice of some trainers, allow the correction to come from the object instead of the owner. These devices are also useful to keep the snacking pooch from napping on furniture that is forbidden.

Just like food stealing, begging is a favorite pastime of hungry puppies with that same reward—food! No dog looks as desperate and appealing as a Yorkie on his twos! Dogs quickly learn that humans love that pose and

that their selfish owners keep the "good food" for themselves. Why would humans dine on kibble alone when they can cook up sausages and kielbasa? Begging is a conditioned response related to a specific stimulus, time, and place. The sounds of the kitchen, cans and bottles opening, crinkling bags, and the smell of food in preparation will excite your dog, and soon the paws are in the air!

Here is the solution to stopping this behavior: Never give in to a beggar, no matter how cute or desperate he may look! You must not reward your Yorkie for jumping, whining, or rubbing his nose into you by giving him that glorious reward—food. By ignoring your dog, you will (eventually) force the behavior into extinction. Note that the behavior likely gets worse before it disappears, so be sure there aren't any softies in the family who will give in to your dog every time he whimpers, "More, please."

POOP ALERT!

Feces eating, aka coprophagia, is, to most humans, the most disgusting behavior that their dog could engage in, yet to the dog it is perfectly normal. Vets have found that diets with low digestibility, containing relatively low levels of fiber and high levels of starch, increase coprophagia. Therefore, high-fiber diets may decrease the likelihood of dogs' eating feces. To discourage this behavior, feed food that is nutritionally complete and in the proper amount. If changes in your Yorkie's diet do not seem to work, and no medical cause can be found for the feces eating, you will have to modify the behavior through environmental control before it becomes a habit.

There are some tricks you can try, such as adding an unpleasant-tasting substance to the feces to make them unpalatable or adding something to the dog's food which

Your Yorkie's bad eating habits could be caused by poor nutrition from his food.

will make it unpleasant tasting after it passes through the dog. The best way to prevent your dog from eating his stool is to make it unavailable—clean up after he eliminates and remove any poop from the yard. If it is not there, he cannot eat it.

Never reprimand your Yorkie for stool eating, as this rarely impresses the dog. Veterinarians recommend distracting the dog while he is in the act of eating feces. Another option is to muzzle the dog when he is in the yard to relieve himself; this usually is effective within thirty to sixty days. Coprophagia most frequently is seen in puppies six to twelve months of age, and usually disappears around the dog's first birthday.

NOTABLE & QUOTABLE

The purpose of puppy classes is for the pups to learn how to learn. The pups get the training along the way, but the training is almost secondary.

—professional trainer Peggy Shunick Duezabou of Helena, Mont.

THE ACTIVE

CHAPTER 12

YORKIE

All dogs require some form of exercise, regardless of the breed. A sedentary lifestyle is as harmful to a dog as it is to a person. Fortunately for the Yorkshire Terrier owner, meeting the breed's requirements is simple.

Regular walks, play sessions with you around the neighborhood, or letting the dog run free in the yard under your supervision are all sufficient forms of exercise for the diminutive Yorkshire Terrier. Not only is exercise essential to keep the dog's body fit, it is essential to his mental well-being. A bored dog will find something to do, which often manifests itself in some type of destructive behavior. In this sense, it is essential for the owner's mental well-being as well!

Whether a dog is trained in the structured environment of a class or alone with his owner at home, there are also many sporting activities that can bring fun and rewards to owner and dog once they have mastered basic control.

TRACKING

Yorkies instinctively use scent to find prey. This same skill allows them to excel at tracking, in which they follow a human-scent trail to locate a glove that's been dropped at the end of the course.

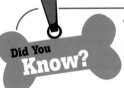

Did You Know? The Fédération Internationale Cynologique is the world kennel club that governs dog shows in Europe and elsewhere around the world.

Before You Begin
Because of the physical demands of sporting activities, a Yorkie puppy shouldn't begin officially training until he is done growing. That doesn't mean, though, that you can't begin socializing him to sports. Talk to your vet about what age is appropriate.

The American Kennel Club started tracking tests in 1937, when the first licensed test took place as part of the Utility level at an obedience trial.

Ten years later, in 1947, the AKC offered the first title, Tracking Dog. It was not until 1980 that the AKC added the Tracking Dog Excellent title, which was followed by the Versatile Surface Tracking title in 1995. The title Champion Tracker is awarded to a dog who has earned all three titles.

Your Yorkie must be at least six months old to participate in a tracking trial, but you can get started teaching him this sport by encouraging him to find objects using scent. You can start with treats and work up to other objects. Get help by joining a tracking class, which will get you started on the right path to training your dog.

OBEDIENCE TRIALS

Obedience trials in the United States trace back to the early 1930s, when organized obedience training was developed to demonstrate how well dog and owner could work together. The pioneer of obedience trials was Mrs. Helen Whitehouse Walker, a Standard Poodle fancier, who designed a series of exercises after the Associated Sheep, Police Army Dog Society of Great Britain. Since the days of Mrs. Walker, obedience trials have grown by leaps and bounds, and today there are over 2,000 trials held in the United States every year, with more than 100,000 dogs competing. Any registered AKC or ILP (Indefinite Listing

Privilege) dog can enter an obedience trial, regardless of conformational disqualifications or neutering.

Obedience trials are divided into three levels of progressive difficulty. At the first level, the Novice, dogs compete for the title Companion Dog; at the intermediate level, the Open, dogs compete for the title Companion Dog Excellent; and at the advanced level, dogs compete for the title Utility Dog. Classes are sub-divided into "A" (for beginners) and "B" (for more experienced handlers). A perfect score at any level is 200, and a dog must score 170 or better to earn a "leg," of which three are needed to earn the title. To earn points, the dog must score more than fifty percent of the available points in

each exercise; the possible points range from twenty to forty.

Once a dog has earned the UD title, he can compete with other proven obedience dogs for the coveted title of Utility Dog Excellent , which requires that the dog win "legs" in ten shows. In 1977, the title Obedience Trial Champion was established by the AKC. Utility Dogs who earn "legs" in Open B and Utility B earn points toward their Obedience Trial Champion title. To become an OTCh., a dog needs to earn 100 points, which requires three first places in Open B and Utility under three different judges.

The Grand Prix of obedience trials, the AKC National Obedience Invitational, gives qualifying Utility Dogs the chance to win

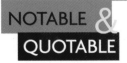

Agility is fun and exciting; provides a great outlet for energy; improves fitness, coordination, and communication; and improves the teamwork between a dog and his handler. Agility dogs run, climb and jump a course of about thirteen to twenty obstacles, racing against time as they demonstrate fitness, focus, and finesse. —dog trainer September Morn

the newest and highest title: National Obedience Champion. Only the top twenty-five ranked obedience dogs, plus any dog ranked in the top three in his breed, are allowed to compete.

AGILITY TRIALS

Agility is one of the most popular dog sports out there. Yorkies are excellent at this activity, which requires speed, precision, and obedience. Training your Yorkie

in agility will boost his confidence and teach him to focus on you.

In agility competition, the dog and handler move through a prescribed course, negotiating a series of obstacles that may include jumps, tunnels, a dog walk, an A-frame, a seesaw, a pause table, and weave poles. Dogs who run through a course without refusing any obstacles, going off course, or knocking down any bars, all within a set time, get a qualifying score. Dogs with a certain number of qualifying scores in their given division (Novice, Open, Excellent, and Mach, at AKC trials) earn an agility title.

Several different organizations recognize agility events. AKC-sanctioned agility events are the most common. The United States Dog Agility Association also sanctions agility trials, as does the United Kennel Club. The rules are different for each of these organizations, but the principles are the same.

When Yorkies compete in agility, they usually jump at a height of only four or eight inches, depending on the height of the

Yorkies aren't as delicate as you may think; they benefit greatly from dog sports.

It used to be that puppies didn't start training class until they were six months old, but by that time, the critical learning period is long gone. Puppy kindergarten—basic training in a casual, nonthreatening environment—is a wonderful way to enhance socialization and learning.

few obstacles in a row, one after another. Once he catches on that this is how agility works, he can run a short course off-leash. One day, you'll see the light go on in his eyes as he figures out that he should look to you for guidance as he runs through a course. Your job will be to tell him which obstacles to take next, using your voice and your body as signals.

dog. With the exception of the jumps, Yorkies are expected to negotiate the other obstacles on the course at the same height and distance as other breeds (the one exception is the pause table, which is lowered). Because each division of agility is subdivided by jump height, Yorkies compete for ribbons against other dogs their own size.

When your Yorkie starts his agility training, he will begin by learning to negotiate each obstacle while on-leash, as you guide him. Eventually, you will steer him through a

RALLY BEHIND RALLY

Rally is a sport that combines competition obedience with elements of agility, but is less demanding than either one of these latter activities. The sport was designed for the average dog owner, and is easier than many other sporting activities.

At a rally event, dogs and handlers are asked to move through ten to twenty different stations, depending on the level of competition. The stations are marked by numbered signs, which tell the handler the

exercise to be performed at this station. The exercises vary from making different types of turns to changing pace.

Dogs can earn rally titles as they get better at the sport and move through the different levels. The titles to strive for are Rally Novice, Rally Advanced, Rally Excellent, and Rally Advanced Excellent.

To get your Yorkie puppy prepared for rally competition, focus on teaching basic obedience, for starters. Your dog must know the five basic obedience cues—sit, stay, come, down, and heel—and perform them well before he's ready for rally. Next, you can enroll your dog in a rally class. Although he must be at least six months of age to compete in rally, you can start training long before his six-month birthday.

Getting kids involved in dog sports with your pup helps to build a bond between the two.

SWIMMING SWEETIES

Yorkies swimming? It seems unlikely. Surprisingly, these little guys love getting their feet wet, especially if they're socialized to water when they're pups. Don't just toss your dog into the water and expect him to swim—build up gradually. Swimming is also very good exercise and is easy on the joints.

Kathy Doheny, a Yorkie owner from Harrisburg, Penn., discovered that her dog, Madisyn, loved to swim while on a trip to Florida. But the dog doesn't just swim—she fully understands the art of poolside relaxation. "Madisyn's favorite thing to do while I'm swimming is to lazily lie on her raft and float around the pool," Doheny says. "If we're

NOTABLE & QUOTABLE

A toy that will keep your Yorkie busy is a plush, soft toy that comes with stuffed animal-like objects that can be removed and replaced inside the outer toy over and over again. The puzzle for your puppy is how to pull the objects out of the larger toy. Some of these "hide-a-toys" come as cubes with different stuffed shapes to put inside or even little stuffed animals like bees or squirrels. Figuring out how to pull these smaller stuffed objects out of the bigger toy will develop your Yorkie's problem-solving skills.

—Mary-Frances Makichen, pet-freelance writer from Washington

outside grilling or just hanging out by the pool, Madisyn will scratch at the side of the pool, her cue to put her on the raft so she can float. If you don't catch the cue, she will bark nonstop and stare at the raft."

Some Yorkies love boating on anything from a ship to a canoe. When sailing out in open water, be sure your dog wears a life jacket that is hooked to a ring in the cockpit. Do not allow your dog to roam the boat.

SHOW DOGS

When you purchase your Yorkshire Terrier, make it clear to the breeder whether you want one just as a lovable companion and pet, or if you hope to be buying a Yorkie with show prospects. No reputable breeder will sell you a young puppy and tell you that he is definitely of show quality, because so much can go wrong during the early months of a puppy's development. If you plan to show, what you will hopefully have acquired is a puppy with "show potential."

To the novice, exhibiting a Yorkshire Terrier in the show ring may look easy, but it takes a lot of hard work and devotion to win at a show such as the prestigious Westminster Kennel Club dog show, not to mention a little luck, too!

The first concept that the canine novice learns when watching a dog show is that each dog first competes against members of its own breed. Once the judge has selected

the best member of each breed (Best of Breed), the chosen dog will compete with other dogs in its group. In AKC-sanctioned dog shows, there are seven groups: Sporting, Working, Hound, Terrier, Toy, Non-sporting and Herding. Yorkies belong in the Toy Group. The dogs chosen first in each group will compete for Best in Show.

The second concept that you must understand is that the dogs are not actually compared against one another. The judge compares each dog against his breed standard, the written description of the ideal specimen that is approved by the AKC. While some early breed standards were indeed based on specific dogs who were famous or popular, many dedicated enthusiasts say that a perfect specimen, as described in the standard, has never walked into a show ring, has never been bred and, to the woe of dog breeders around the

Sports are physically demanding. Have your vet do a full examination of your Yorkie to rule out joint problems, heart disease, eye aliments, and other maladies. Once you get the all-clear healthwise, start having fun in your new sporting life!

SMART TIP!

The man with Alzheimer's disease wouldn't talk to anyone, not even his daughter. Then Honey Bunny arrived. As the little Yorkshire Terrier sat on his lap, he petted her and began telling her about his childhood on a farm where his family raised pigs. As his daughter listened, tears rolled down her face. She had never heard any of these stories. For the next four months before he died, she wrote down everything her father said during Bunny's weekly visits.

Yorkies have the right stuff when it comes to animal-assisted activities (pets visiting people) and animal-assisted therapy (programs tailored to an individual's emotional or medical needs). They love to be petted and sweet-talked, and are just the right size to sit on beds and nestle in laps.

An encounter with a therapy dog started Pat Shaeffer of Rockledge, Fla., on the road to therapy visits. "My husband was in the hospital having a screw put in a broken hip, and a woman with a therapy dog came into his room," Shaeffer says. "We talked for a long time, and she directed me to the president of Space Coast Therapy Dogs in Merritt Island, Fla. Things snowballed after that. That's why I have four therapy Yorkies now." Those Yorkies are Gypsy Blue (Blue), a ten-year-old female retired show dog; Stormin' Badberry (Stormy), a seven-year-old male retired show dog; Aces High Vito (Ace), an eight-year-old male retired show dog; and the aforementioned Honey Bunny (Bunny), who is eight years old.

Taking turns, they visit nursing homes, assisted-living homes, rehab centers, senior citizen centers, cancer care centers, and schools for children with physical and mental challenges. "After a dog is registered for twelve months, he's eligible to be tested in a hospital to become part of the hospital's therapy-dog program," Shaeffer says. "Some of us are also certified to visit hospice patients in their homes or private facilities."

globe, does not exist. Breeders attempt to get as close to this ideal as possible with every litter, but theoretically the "perfect" dog is so elusive that it is impossible. (And if the "perfect" dog were born, breeders and judges probably would never agree that he was indeed "perfect.")

If you are interested in exploring the world of conformation, your best bet is to join your local breed club or the national (or parent) club, which is the Yorkshire Terrier Club of America. These clubs often host both regional and national specialties, shows only for Yorkies, which can include conformation as well as obedience and field trials. Even if you have no intention of competing with your Yorkie, a specialty is a like a festival for lovers of the breed who congregate to share their favorite topic: Yorkies!

Clubs also send out newsletters, and some organize training days and seminars in order that people may learn more about their chosen breed. To locate the breed club closest to you, contact the AKC, which furnishes the rules and regulations for all of these events, plus general dog registration and other basic requirements of dog ownership.

it's a Fact

In 1978, a Yorkshire Terrier named Ch. Cede Higgins, owned by Barbara and Charles Switzer, won Best in Show at the annual Westminster Kennel Club Dog Show!

CHAPTER 13

RESOURCES

To find more information about this popular dog breed, contact the following organizations. They will be glad to help you dig deeper into the world of the Yorkshire Terrier.

American Kennel Club: The AKC website offers information and links to conformation, tracking, rally, obedience and agility programs, and member clubs: www.akc.org

Canadian Kennel Club: Our northern neighbor's oldest kennel club is similar to the AKC and the United Kennel Club in the states: www.ckc.ca

North American Dog Agility Council: This site provides links to clubs, trainers, and agility trainers in the United States and Canada: www.nadac.com

United Kennel Club: The UKC offers several of the events offered by the AKC, including agility, conformation, and obedience. In addition, the UKC offers competitions in hunting and dog sport (companion and protective events). Both the UKC and the AKC offer programs for juniors, ages two to eighteen: www.ukcdogs.com

United States Dog Agility Association: The USDAA has information on training, clubs, and events in the United States, Canada, Mexico, and overseas: www.usdaa.com

it's a **Fact**

The **American Kennel Club** was started in 1884. It is America's oldest kennel club. The **United Kennel Club** is the second oldest in the United States. It began registering dogs in 1898.

Yorkshire Terrier Club of America: The YTCA is a nonprofit organization with more than 500 members across the country: www.ytca.org

Yorkshire Terrier National Rescue: This organization was founded in 1997 to find homes for Yorkies who were abandoned: www.yorkshireterrierrescue.com

United Yorkie Rescue: This is an organization that rescues Yorkshire Terriers from animal shelters so that appropriate families can adopt them: www.unitedyorkierescue.org

BOARDING

So you want to take a family vacation—and you want to include all members of the family. You usually make arrangements for accommodations ahead of time anyway, but this is especially important when traveling with a dog. You do not want to make an overnight stop at the only place around for miles and find out that they do not allow dogs. Also, you do not want to reserve a room for your family without confirming that you are traveling with a dog because, if it is against the hotel's policy, you may not have a place to stay.

Alternatively, if you are traveling and choose not to bring your Yorkie, you will have to make arrangements for him. Some options are to bring him to a family member or a neighbor or to have a trusted friend stop by often or stay at your house, or to bring your dog to a reputable boarding kennel.

If you choose to board him at a kennel, you should visit in advance to see the facilities, how clean they are, and where the dogs are kept. Talk to some of the employees and see how they treat the dogs—do they spend time with the dogs, play with them, exercise them, etc.? Also

find out the kennel's policy on vaccinations and what they require. This is for all of the dogs' safety because when dogs are kept together, there is a greater risk of diseases being passed from dog to dog.

Taking a trip with your terrier doesn't have to be a big to-do as long as you prepare in advance.

HOME STAFFING

For the Yorkie parent who works all day, a pet sitter or dog walker may be the perfect solution for the lonely terrier longing for a midday stroll. Dog owners can approach local high schools or community centers if they don't know of a neighbor who is interested in a part-time commitment. Interview potential dog walkers and consider their experience with dogs, as well as your Yorkie's rapport with the candidate. (Yorkies are excellent judges of character, unless there's liver involved.) Always check references before entrusting your dog and home to a new dog walker.

For an owner's long-term absence, such as a three-day business trip or a one-week vacation, many terrier owners welcome the services of a pet-sitter. It's usually less stressful on the dog to stay home with a pet sitter than to be boarded in a kennel. Pet sitters also may be more affordable than a week's stay at a full-service doggie day care.

Pet sitters must be even more reliable than dog walkers because the dog is depending on his surrogate owner for all of his needs for an extended period. Owners are advised to hire a certified pet sitter through the National Association of Professional Pet Sitters, which can be accessed online at www.petsitters.org. NAPPS provides online and toll-free pet sitter locator services. The nonprofit organization only certifies serious-minded, professional individuals who are knowledgeable in canine behavior, nutrition, health, and safety. Always keep your Yorkie's best interest at heart when planning a trip.

If you need to be away for more than a few hours, consider hiring a pet sitter to watch over your Yorkies.

SCHOOL'S IN SESSION

Puppy kindergarten, which is usually open to puppies between three to six months of age, allows puppies to learn and socialize with other dogs and people in a structured setting. Classes help your Yorkie enjoy going places with you, and help your dog become a well-behaved member at public gatherings that include other dogs. They prepare him for adult obedience classes, as well as for life.

The problem with most puppy kindergarten classes is that they only occur one night a week. What about during the rest of the week?

If you're at home all week, you may be able to find other places to take your puppy, but you have to be careful about dog parks and other places where just any dog can go. An experience with a bully can undo all the good your classes have done, or worse, end in tragedy.

If you work, your puppy may be home alone all day, a tough situation for an energetic Yorkshire Terrier. Chances are he can't hold himself that long, so your potty training will be undermined unless you're just aiming to teach him to use an indoor potty. And chances are, by the time you come home,

SMART TIP!

Remember to keep your dog's leash slack when interacting with other dogs. It is not unusual for a dog to pick out one or two canine neighbors to dislike. If you know there's bad blood, step off to the side and put a barrier, such as a parked car, between the dogs. If there are no barriers to be had, move to the side of the walkway, cue your dog to sit, stay, and watch you until his nemesis passes; then continue your walk.

he'll be bursting with energy and you may start thinking that he's hyperactive.

The answer? Doggie day care. Most larger cities have some sort of day care, whether it's a boarding kennel that keeps your dog in a run or a full-service day care that offers training, play time, and even spa facilities. They range from a person who keeps a few dogs at his home to a state-of-the-art facility built just for the purpose. Many of the more sophisticated doggie day cares offer webcams so you can see your dog throughout the day.

Look for:
- escape-proof facilities, including a buffer between the dogs and any doors
- inoculation requirements for new dogs
- midday meals for young dogs
- obedience training (if offered), using reward-based methods
- safe and comfortable time-out areas for sleeping
- screening of dogs for aggression
- small groups of similar sizes and ages
- toys and playground equipment, such as tunnels
- trained staff, with an adequate number to supervise the dogs (no more than ten to fifteen dogs per person)
- webcam

CAR TRAVEL

You should accustom your Yorkie to riding in a car at an early age. You may or may not take him in the car often, but at the very least he will need to go to the vet and you do not want these trips to be traumatic for the dog or troublesome for you. The safest way for a dog to ride in the car is in his crate. If he uses a crate in the house, you can use the same crate for travel.

Another option is a specially made safety harness for dogs, which straps the dog in much like a seat belt would. Do not let the dog roam loose in the vehicle—this is very dangerous! If you should stop short, your dog can be thrown and injured. If the dog starts climbing on you and pestering you while you are driving, you will not be able to concen-

trate on the road. It is an unsafe situation for everyone—human and canine.

For long trips, be prepared to stop to let your dog relieve himself. Take along with you whatever you need to clean up after him, including some paper towels and perhaps some old bath towels for use should he have an accident in the car or suffer from motion sickness.

IDENTIFICATION

Your Yorkie is your valued companion and friend. That is why you always keep a close eye on him and you have made sure that he cannot escape from the yard or wriggle out of his collar and run away from you. However, accidents can happen and there may come a time when your dog unexpectedly gets separated from you. If this should occur, the first thing on your mind will be finding him. Proper identification, including an ID tag, a tattoo, and possibly a microchip, will increase the chances of his being returned to you safely and quickly.

An ID tag on a collar or harness is the primary means of pet identification (and ID licenses are required in many communities, anyway). Although inexpensive and easy to read, collars and ID tags can come off or be taken off.

A microchip doesn't get lost. Containing a unique ID number which can be read by a scanner, the microchip is embedded under the pet's skin. It's invaluable for identifying lost or stolen pets. However, to be effective, the chip must be registered in a national database, and smart owners will be sure their contact info is kept up-to-date. Additionally, not every shelter or veterinary clinic has a scanner, nor do most folks who might pick up and try to return a lost pet.

Best bet: Get both!

Did You Know? Some communities have created regular dog runs and separate spaces for small dogs. These small dog runs are ideal for introducing puppies to the dog park experience. The runs are smaller, the participants are smaller, and their owners are often more vigilant because they are used to watching out for their fragile companions

REPLY CARD FOR A FREE GUIDE!

Send in this card and receive a FREE Guide to Flea & Tick Prevention.

(While supplies last)

Thank you for purchasing one of BowTie's exceptional books. We are sincerely interested in any comments you may have on your Smart Owner's Guide® breed book purchase and thank you for your time.

COMMENTS:

1. Name _____

   Address _____

   City/State/ZIP _____

   E-mail address _____
   ☐ Yes, I want to receive special e-mail promotions from carefully selected third parties.

2. Age: ☐ 18   ☐ 19-25   ☐ 26-45   ☐ 46-55   ☐ Over 55

3. Location of purchase: City_____ State_____

4. What other topics are of interest to you?
   ☐ Breeds   ☐ Training   ☐ Cats   ☐ Birds   ☐ Critters   ☐ Farming/Gardening   ☐ Green Living

For more information about BowTie Press, visit bowtiepress.com

2011YT

BOWTIE PRESS
PO BOX 6050
MISSION VIEJO, CA 92690-9818